Harvest

C O O K B O O K

By Monica Musetti-Carlin and Mary Elizabeth Roarke

Hatherleigh Press is committed to preserving and protecting the natural resources of the Earth. Environmentally responsible and sustainable practices are embraced within the company's mission statement.

Hatherleigh Press is a member of the Publishers Earth Alliance, committed to preserving and protecting the natural resources of the planet while developing a sustainable business model for the book publishing industry.

This book was edited and designed in the village of Hobart, New York. Hobart is a community that has embraced books and publishing as a component of its livelihood. There are several unique bookstores in the village. For more information, please visit www.hobartbookvillage.com.

www.hatherleighpress.com

Library of Congress Cataloging-in-Publication Data
Musetti-Carlin, Monica.
   Country comfort. Harvest / Monica Musetti-Carlin and Mary Elizabeth Roarke.
      p. cm.
   ISBN 978-1-57826-359-2 (pbk.: alk. paper) 1. Cooking, American. 2. Autumn. I. Roarke, Mary Elizabeth, II. Title. III. Title: Harvest.

TX715.M962 2010
641.5973–dc22
                              2010023669

Country Comfort: Harvest is available for bulk purchase, special promotions, and premiums. For information on reselling and special purchase opportunities, call 1-800-528-2550 and ask for the Special Sales Manager.

Cover design by Nick Macagnone
Interior design by Nick Macagnone
Cover photography by Catarina Astrom
Illustration on pages 1, 25, 67, and 121 by Judith Cheng

10 9 8 7 6 5 4 3 2 1

DISCLAIMER
Any similarities to existing recipes are purely coincidental.

I dedicate this book to my wonderful son Matt, who knows how to appreciate good food.

Monica

I dedicate this book to my Mom and Dad for sharing their love of baking and cooking; to Nicole for sharing her culinary passion; to my husband Dennis and our other children Elizabeth, Dennis, and Christian, thank you for your constant love and support.

Mary Elizabeth

Thanks to Matthew Carlin for his computer prowess and research skills.

Thanks to Nicole Roarke for putting into words our suggestions for the Chef's Tips section.

Thank you to all of our creative home cooks who shared their families' favorite recipes.

Thank you for supporting our efforts and sending out our recipe request to your network of chefs:

Erik Murnighan, The French Culinary Institute, New York, NY

Chef Michael S. Meshel, New York Guild of Chefs, Inc.

Chef Roland A. Iadanza, www.pastapeopleny.com

Thanks to the patient staff at Starbucks in Bayport and Borders in Bohemia, NY, where we sat for countless hours, drinking great coffee and listening to sweet music as we finalized this book.

Table Of Contents

Foreword

The warmest, richest flavors and feelings are enjoyed at harvest time, when we regale in the bounty of the season by celebrating with flavorful and hearty foods. Harvest time is a special treat for the chefs and cooks in all of us. Root vegetables abound and, along with the final crops of corn and summer vegetables, bring the true bounty of traditional American cuisine to the table. In the fall the livestock is especially rich in flavor from a generous summer feeding and the cheeses are decadent and delicious.

Mary Elizabeth and Monica have compiled an exceptional variety of recipes for the harvest season. It is clear that these are recipes from the heart. They have blended many traditional dishes with wonderful modern recipes, crafting meals that will quickly become favorites. The contributors to this book are as varied as the recipes you will find within. I am proud to say that some of these contributing chefs are good friends of mine, and I am sure that when you try their recipes you will find the quality to be exceptional. With this book, you have the rare opportunity to peek into the heart of the culinarian.

The traditions and family remembrances recounted along with many of these recipes are inspiring. With *Country Comfort: Harvest,* I found myself transported back to the warm family meals of my youth.

Cooking and baking have always been a great unifying factor of the American family. When gathered around the dinner table, we have the opportunity to share stories about our day and appreciate a meal prepared with love and skill. Through this book, you are going to be transported back to a time when dinner was the highlight of the family's day. Follow the caring guidance of these two dedicated women and use this book as an opportunity to recreate that experience for your family and friends.

Whether you are a seasoned chef or a home cook, you will find these recipes are a great motivator for you to explore the variety of foods available at the harvest time. In these days of fast-food and take-out meals, we can appreciate the rich and loving recipes that Mary Elizabeth and Monica have gathered for this book.

It is now your turn to start creating memories and enjoying the moments that they will inspire. Keep in mind that creativity is part of cooking and baking. Once you are comfortable with the recipes, don't be shy—let yourself feel inspired to try out your ideas and make these meals your own. Your family and friends will remember them fondly.

I am proud to be part of this book and I congratulate Mary Elizabeth and Monica for a cookbook that will be cherished for years to come.

—*Executive Chef Michael S. Meshel*
President, New York Guild of Chefs, Inc.
Smithtown, New York

Note to the Reader

In some ways, it seems writing *Country Comfort: Harvest* was meant to be. We both have a strong love for baking, cooking, and sharing recipes and traditions. Mary Elizabeth's family has a background in baking: relatives on her father's side started a bakery when they had arrived in America from Germany. As Mary Elizabeth was growing up, she had the best of both worlds, because her Dad loved to cook and her Mom loved to bake. A science lover, Mary Elizabeth naturally gravitated toward baking, completing a Baking & Pastry arts program at a local culinary school. Now, she does catering with her daughter Nicole, who is a chef.

Monica has always loved to write and, as a self-proclaimed "memory keeper," has been collecting stories, memories, and recipes for years. By now, she has a story or recipe for just about any topic imaginable. Her love of cooking is inspired by her mother and Monica's years of traveling throughout the United States and Europe, with her husband, collecting obscure cookbooks, and replicating the tastes and flavors she has encountered.

Once we decided to write *Country Comfort: Harvest,* we immediately began reaching out to individuals to gather stories and recipes. We then expanded our search by hosting a tea party to reach a wider range of individuals and contacted organizations, including local farms, restaurants, chefs, caterers, green markets, farm stands, craft fairs, culinary schools, and individuals with successful home-based businesses that have cooking at their heart. The result is a wide selection of delicious, meaningful recipes from all over the country. Finally, we opened our personal "treasure chests" of our families' favorite recipes to share with you, our readers. Any unidentified recipes throughout this book have been passed along by Mary Elizabeth or Monica. Since the beginning of this project, we have added many more comfort food recipes to our stories. We have also added older recipes with new healthy variations incorporating locally harvested herbs, fruits and vegetables.

Country Comfort: Harvest has something for any cook, no matter their level of experience. The diverse selection of our contributors has produced recipes that appeal to all types of cooks: the novice who cannot yet deviate from a recipe, but likes to cook and is seeking out unique meals; the seasoned, self-taught cook who uses a recipe as their basic format and then alters or substitutes as they go along; and the new chef who looks to recipes for inspiration and then allows their creativity to take charge.

Our hope is that *Country Comfort: Harvest* will become a valuable resource that you will want to experiment with, learn from, and enjoy. Each recipe here is someone else's favorite and we know that they would only share their very best ones with you. As you walk through the following pages, we urge you to find comfort in knowing that the recipes you try hold a special place at someone's table. We expect that, someday, they will be your favorites, too. Enjoy these recipes and, one day, hand them down to your own future generations.

—*Mary Elizabeth and Monica*

Introduction:
Passing on Traditions Through Food

The tradition of getting together with family or friends for annual celebrations generates lasting feelings of closeness and warmth. We create our own comfort zones by repeating these familiar activities. It is the "we always … " the "my family does this … ," or "every year we get together and go … " that strengthens our mutual relationships and sense of self. These are chances to share stories, jokes, and, of course, recipes.

Most of us never really think about our traditions. Yet our traditions are as unique and varied as we are. Yours may be on a small scale, such as a trip to the country to go apple-picking, where you may take in the local ambience, visit a couple of farm stands and later, cook up the goodies you have found. Perhaps you have larger scale traditions, like family reunions where everybody prepares their specialties and shares prized recipes, sometimes handed down through the generations. Large or small, traditions offer an opportunity to spend time with people we care about in order to renew our relationships.

If you do not yet have a tradition, there is no time like the present to start one. Sharing food and fun is the perfect beginning. Fall is a particularly special time for traditions, when a fun event to brighten the shorter, chillier days is always welcome. As the evenings start to turn brisk in September, Monica thinks back to her family reunions, where everyone would gather around a huge bonfire to toast marshmallows and catch up with each other. As kids, once school started, we would start our mornings with warm oatmeal topped with fresh apples and cinnamon, and then, toting a lunch box with homemade peanut butter and jam, line up for the school bus.

Each month of the season has its own distinctive fresh produce. September says apples. We bundle up on weekends in warm sweaters and socks to go apple-picking, loading up our red Radio Flyer wagon with McIntosh, Macoun, and Rome apples and fresh pears still warm from the autumn sun. Later, we return home hungry for homemade minestrone soup made from the last remnants of our garden tomatoes, zucchini, basil, and peppers, which we pair with freshly made bread and cheese. For dessert, we will enjoy hot cider and apple treats bought from the farm stands we visited during the day's trip.

If September says apples, October shouts pumpkins—and pumpkins scream fun for all ages. On annual trips to the pumpkin fields, you will find a plethora of bright orange pumpkins of all shapes and sizes just ripe for picking. Tall and trim, fat and round— you pick the one that speaks to you. Try to choose several different sizes. The smallest can be used as mini dessert bowls, the larger ones for carving, and the medium-sized pumpkins are perfect for baking breads, cakes, bisques, and of course, pumpkin pie. They also make great soup tureens.

As autumn winds down, the vibrant reds, yellows, and oranges change to blues and grays, and the scent of fireplaces fills the chilled air. It is now time to take stock and make stock. Part of your annual fall cleaning should include an inventory of your pantry to make sure you are prepared for inclement weather—you never know when a snowstorm may hit. Make sure you have plenty of jams for breakfast, along with tomato sauce, pickles, corn relishes, chutneys, and salsas for any impromptu dinner parties. Harvest, dry, and store your garden herbs, and then prepare and freeze fish, chicken, meat, and vegetable stocks for savory soups and gravies. Check your dishes, cutlery, and glassware at this time, well before the holidays, to make sure there are no chips or missing place settings. Bring light and color into the house by setting a pretty table even for everyday meals. Alternate sets of dishes, bright cloth napkins, and tablecloths, and add a seasonal centerpiece.

Create your own tradition, be it simple or extravagant. Most importantly, like good food or wine, savor your traditions year after year and enjoy them with friends and family.

Part I

BREAKFAST & BRUNCH

Breakfast & Brunch

Nutritionally speaking, breakfast is the most important meal of the day: studies have shown that kids do better in school when they eat a healthy breakfast. Breakfast is also important socially. The beginning of a new day provides the perfect chance to congregate with the rest of the household and discuss everyone's daily plans before going off in our different directions. When we are solo, the first meal of the day can also be a time to meditate, plan the day ahead, or enjoy the news over a hot cup of freshly ground coffee or steaming mug of tea.

Weekday breakfasts may simply mean cold cereal and fresh milk, but weekends are a different story. On weekends, we often have more time to prepare and savor our meals. In some homes, the scent of bacon wafting through the house will beckon those still in bed to get up and greet the new morning. For others, the perfect breakfast includes two eggs over easy or a fluffy western omelet, hot oatmeal with cinnamon and fruit, toast with jam, crumb cake, or harvest muffins. Complete your meal with a cup of coffee or tea with milk and honey and you are all set to languidly eat while lingering over the Sunday newspaper. Brunch is another story: you can incorporate pasta dishes like savory pumpkin ravioli along with your usual breakfast fare.

Breakfast connoisseurs in Vermont may feast on blueberry pancakes dripping with local dark amber maple syrup, while in Manhattan, they may have bagels with a "schmear," or granola, fruit, and yogurt in California.

Using farm fresh eggs, garden herbs, local veggies, cheeses, and preserves, and homemade bread for French toast will make waking up as memorable as a glorious sunrise. Breakfast is not a meal to be skipped or taken lightly. It sets the tone for the rest of the day…and every new day sets the tone for the rest of our lives.

Autumnal Crepes

Monica

Makes 12 crepes

This is a pretty basic crepe recipe I discovered when I was first married. I would impress my friends at brunch with these sweet and light creations once the September days started getting cooler and our camping and beach weekends dwindled. We would turn our activities indoors as the weather grew chilly and the leaves changed outdoors, playing music in front of the fireplace, eating and laughing all day. The colorful red of the cranberries and the bright yellow of the preserves in this recipe truly reflect autumn's jewel tones. To alter the flavor while staying in the same color palette, you can also use cherry or apricot preserves. I like using pignoli nuts because they are as light as the crepe itself. My old friend John told me that adding orange juice to any recipe makes the sauce more pungent, which is certainly the case with these delicious crepes.

Crepes

⅔ cup milk

2 eggs

1 tablespoon canola oil

½ cup flour

1 teaspoon sugar

¼ teaspoon salt

Filling

1 (8 ounce) package
of cream cheese, softened

8 ounces salted butter

¼ cup honey

1½ teaspoons grated orange
rind

2 tablespoons orange-flavored
liqueur

⅛ cup cranberries, whole
unsweetened

1 cup pignoli nuts, lightly
toasted

⅔ cups orange marmalade

Blend milk, eggs, oil, flour, sugar, and salt until smooth.

Lightly grease the grill. Once heated, put in 2 tablespoons of the batter, quickly forming into a circle. Lightly brown one side, and then the other. Continue until all the batter is used up.

Separate each crepe with a single piece of waxed paper and set aside while you make the filling.

Combine cream cheese, butter, honey, orange rind and orange liqueur and beat. Fold in pignoli nuts.

Spoon 1½ tablespoons of the mixture into each crepe, fold over opposite sides of the crepe overlapping slightly.

Butter a shallow baking dish and put in crepes, dotting each with butter. Bake uncovered about 10 minutes at 350°F.

Sauce

Heat orange marmalade, cranberries, remaining orange juice, and butter.

Stir constantly but gently until preserves are melted and cranberries just burst.

Add in the rest of the orange liqueur, stir, then spoon over filled crepes, sprinkling the rest of the pignoli nuts on top.

Use your regular pancake recipe and add various fruit and nut combinations to add seasonal flavor. Fold into your batter any of these delicious additions: ¼ cup pureed pumpkin, chopped walnuts, raisins, ⅛ teaspoon cinnamon; blueberries; bananas with chopped pecans; apples with chopped walnuts and raisins; peaches with dried cranberries.

French Toast

Dorothy Acierno *(Bayport, NY)*

> I have been making this recipe for many years—first with my children and now with my grandchildren. I think everyone in my town has made it by now because I have passed it along so many times. It is always a crowd pleaser! After you serve it, get ready to soak up the compliments!

12 slices good quality bread
1 cup brown sugar
1 stick sweet butter, melted
2 tablespoons corn syrup (light or dark)
6 eggs
1½ cups whole milk
1 teaspoon vanilla
Pinch of salt

Mix sugar, butter, and corn syrup together in a bowl, and pour into a buttered 13-inch x 9-inch pan.

In a separate bowl, beat eggs with milk, vanilla, and salt.

Soak each slice of bread separately and place on top of the sugar mixture, close together.

Cover with plastic wrap and let sit overnight in the fridge.

Cover with tin foil and bake at 350°F for 30 to 40 minutes until golden brown.

Warm Fruit Compote

Monica

> French toast, though delicious, should be balanced with a
> healthier component, such as fruit. On a fall morning when
> apples and pears are plentiful, I like to make a stove-top warm
> fruit compote. The scent of it simmering makes your mouth
> water, and even the kids want to know what is cooking. You can
> start off the compote with water and sugar, or fruit juice and a
> thickener like arrowroot, and then stir in your favorite fruits.

2 cups apple juice, 1 cup water
¼ cup sugar
2 Bosc pears, skinned and sliced thick
2 Red Delicious apples, skinned and sliced thick
¼ cup dried apricots, coarsely chopped
¼ cup raisins, coarsely chopped
A dash each of ground cloves and cinnamon

Boil the juice, water, and sugar until syrupy.

Add fruit and spices and simmer for 5 to 10 minutes until soft, not
mushy.

Serve alongside the French toast.

Popovers

Jane Emel *(Blue Point, NY)*
<u>Makes 6 large popovers</u>

> The key to this one is room-temperature eggs and a special pan for popovers (you can purchase at a kitchenware store, or if unavailable, custard cups on a cookie sheet can be successful, too). Warm ingredients and a hot pan help the popovers "pop" larger.

3 eggs, room-temperature
1½ cups flour
1½ cups milk
½ teaspoon salt
1 tablespoon butter melted

Preheat oven to 450°F. Spray pan with cooking spray.

Preheat popover pan for a few minutes.

Beat eggs slightly and add remaining ingredients. Beat until smooth (It is helpful if you mix in a bowl that has a pour spout to fill the pan and quickly close oven).

Fill popover cups ¾ full. Bake for 15 minutes at 450°F, and then lower to 325°F. Continue baking for approximately 25 minutes until golden (do not open oven until done).

Mom's Old Fashioned Zucchini Bread

Chef Lee Stevens *(East Patchogue, NY)*

This is a great recipe from upstate New York, where zucchini is plentiful in the fall. Even though it calls for a cup of oil, I have added additional nutritious ingredients to improve the overall health benefits of the dish. I have had some luck in replacing the white flour and white sugar with whole wheat flour and raw sugar. You can also replace some of the oil with applesauce and/or buttermilk, but this will change the taste. This is one of the few dishes that I have made year in and year out for over forty years.

3 cups flour
1 cup sugar
1 teaspoon baking powder
1 teaspoon baking soda
1 tablespoon cinnamon
½ teaspoon salt
½ cup wheat germ
¼ cup or more of ground flax seed or whole flax seed
½ cup chopped walnuts
½ cup raisins
2 cups grated zucchini
2 eggs
1 cup vegetable oil

Mix the wet ingredients well and add to the dry ingredients until well moistened.

Lightly grease a pie pan with butter, coat with flour, and pour mixture in.

Bake at 300°F for 1 hour, at which point start testing by inserting a knife into the bread. When it comes out dry, remove from oven and cool on a rack. Try and remove the bread as soon as it is done, so, it does not become too dry.

Roasted Root Vegetable Hash with Crispy Pancetta and Poached Eggs

Chef Nicole Roarke *(Blue Point, NY)*

2 sweet potatoes or yams
2 large carrots
3 medium parsnips
1 butternut squash
1 acorn squash
1 rutabaga
4-6 large Red Bliss potatoes
2 cups blended oil (see Chef's Tips)
1 tablespoon each curry and paprika
1 teaspoon cumin
½ teaspoon nutmeg
3 tablespoons honey
½ cup fresh sage leaves, minced
1 cup whole, peeled garlic cloves, roasted
1 pound pancetta
8 eggs
3 tablespoons white vinegar
Salt and pepper to taste

Preheat oven to 400°F.

In a small bowl, make a spice mix of curry, paprika, cumin, and nutmeg. Set aside.

Wash, peel, and chop all root vegetables into ½-inch cubes (peeling the potatoes is optional).

Place sweet potatoes, butternut and acorn squash, and rutabaga in a large mixing bowl with ½ cup of oil and salt and pepper to taste. Add 1 tablespoon of your spice mix. Toss and coat evenly.

Pour vegetable mix onto baking sheet and spread into one even layer.

Roast in the oven for at least 1 hour until all vegetables are fork tender and crispy on the outside.

To ensure even browning, use a metal spatula to flip vegetables during roasting.

Repeat the above process with the Red Bliss potatoes, using only 1 teaspoon of the spice mix.

Repeat the above process with carrots and parsnips using only 1 teaspoon of the spice mix and ¼ cup of oil. Note: Roasting the vegetables separately is the key to ensure that they cook evenly.

Dice pancetta into ½-inch cubes. Place large sauté pan on stove top over medium-high flame. When pan is hot, add pancetta. Stir constantly until it crisps up and begins to brown.

Place all vegetables and pancetta into a large bowl, and toss with honey, sage, garlic, salt, and pepper to taste.

Serve alongside poached eggs.

To Roast Garlic

Place cup of whole, peeled garlic cloves and ¾ cup of blended oil into a small saucepan over a low flame.

Allow garlic to slowly simmer until golden brown and soft. This takes approximately 25 to 30 minutes.

To Poach Eggs Perfectly

In a medium saucepan, bring water to a simmer, and then turn heat down slightly to achieve the perfect poaching temperature of 180 °F. By sight, this is slightly under a simmer, and you will see little bubbles just at the edge of the saucepan on the surface of the water. Then add 3 tablespoons of white vinegar. Working with the eggs, one by one, crack each egg into a small glass cup (such as a ramekin or custard cup). Hold the cup just above the surface of the water, and gently slide the egg into the water. Using a spoon, gently nudge the whites closer to the yolk to reinforce its shape. Cover pan for 3 to 5 minutes.

Then remove the eggs with a slotted spoon. Repeat the above process with the remaining eggs.

Perfect poached eggs should have fully cooked whites and runny yolk. Poaching eggs is another technique that takes practice, but once you have mastered it, you will find it is easier than anticipated.

Applesauce Loaves

(Serve with Cream Cheese Icing or Maple Walnut Butter)
Monica

> When my husband and I were first married in 1977, we did quite a bit of camping. On one trip, we discovered a glorious apple orchard on the grounds of SUNY New Paltz, and zealously began apple picking. Back at the campsite, we concocted endless recipes with our camping buddies. The baking continued for at least another week after we had returned home. One of our favorites was the recipe for applesauce loaves.
>
> Every autumn, I can still recall the scents, colors, and flavors of the different kinds of apples we had picked, and baking this special loaf brings memories rushing back. I now invite family members and friends to share the joyful experience. My nephew even bakes my applesauce cake for his co-workers, and my sister's third grade class makes my applesauce every September.

½ cup butter
¾ cup sugar
¼ cup light brown sugar
1 egg, beaten
1 teaspoon vanilla
1½ cups applesauce
1 cup whole wheat flour
1 cup white flour
2⅛ teaspoons baking soda
½ teaspoon cinnamon
¼ teaspoon ground cloves
1 cup chopped walnuts
1 cup raisins

Preheat oven to 350°F. Cream butter and sugars, add egg and vanilla, and add the rest of the ingredients in the order above. Bake in 3 buttered loaf pans, filling half way for 30 to 35 minutes, or until a skewer comes out dry (test after 30 minutes as ovens vary).

Applesauce

Monica

> I use this recipe for my applesauce. My substantial apple harvest yields quarts of homemade applesauce, so I freeze whatever is not used immediately for future cakes. When giving my loaf cake as a gift, I often accompany it with a jar of applesauce. I have received so much positive feedback from friends and family that I have begun to sell the cake and applesauce to individuals, as well as at fairs and festivals. Both will soon be available in local specialty shops and on the internet.

10 pounds apples, the more varieties the better
1 cup water
⅛ to ¼ cup sugar
⅛ to ¼ cup lemon juice, in increments
Sprinkling of cinnamon to flavor, in increments

Wash, core, and cut up the first 3 pounds of apples. Place apples in a large sauce pot and add water barely to cover. Simmer. As those apples begin to soften, keep adding more (as many as your large sauce pot will fit; I use about 15 to 30 apples, depending on the variety or sizes of the apple). In increments, add more lemon juice, sugar, and cinnamon, relative to the increased amount of apples that you have added to the pot. Once all the apples are soft (this takes about an hour), they are ready to be made into sauce in your blender. Immediately use the necessary amount to bake applesauce cake. Can or freeze the remainder for future use in sterilized jars. Store in the refrigerator for up to 2 weeks or the freezer for up to one year (fill mason jars ⅛ inch from the top, so not to explode).

Cream Cheese Icing

6 ounces cream cheese, softened

½ cup butter, softened

2 tablespoons whole milk

2 teaspoons vanilla extract

2 cups confectioner's sugar

Beat the cream cheese with the butter.

Alternately, add the confectioner's sugar with the milk and vanilla until the consistency is spreadable.

Maple Walnut Butter

Monica

I make this butter as an extra special touch to complement my applesauce loaf when I give it as gifts to my co-workers. You can mix all sorts of flavors into butter and use it on breads, vegetables, or pancakes.

1 stick salted butter
¼ cup maple syrup
½ cup walnuts, finely chopped

Add maple syrup and walnuts to softened butter.
Keep refrigerated until ready to use.

We typically buy Vermont maple syrup in the fall, which is a staple at local farm stands, sold in old fashioned jugs or in glistening maple-shaped bottles. Vermont maple syrup is actually harvested in late February through early April. As with the peak of their fall foliage, Vermonters say it is hard to tell just when the sugaring will peak. Heading west toward Minnesota, the harvest goes from mid-March through mid-April, and maple syrup drizzled on snow is a delicacy.

Frittata

6 eggs
2 cups mixed vegetables: red, yellow, orange peppers, 1 small yellow onion, mushrooms, and zucchini, all sliced very thin
2 tablespoons fresh chopped parsley
3 cloves garlic, diced as small as possible
1½ cups shredded cheddar cheese
Extra virgin olive oil

Lightly coat a round baking dish with olive oil, beat the eggs, and pour into the baking dish, layering in your garlic, veggies, and parsley. Then cover with shredded cheese.

Bake at 350°F for 10 to 15 minutes, making sure the egg mixture is fully cooked in the center. Slice like a pie and serve immediately.

Simple Alternate Method

If you are in a hurry, this method produces a delicious frittata in a third of the time. Using an oven-proof skillet, partially cook all the vegetables that you are planning to use on your stove-top over medium heat with 1 teaspoon of olive oil. Pour the whisked eggs and cheese mixture directly into the skillet. Place in the oven under the broiler until the frittata is lightly golden and the eggs are fully set (approximately 5 minutes).

Fruit Granola

Anthony Noberini *(Brooklyn, NY)*

Makes 5 cups

> This granola recipe is quite simple and can be adapted to incorporate most dried fruits. It is great when served with yogurt and seasonal fresh fruits, like grapes and apples. It also makes a great homemade gift for any occasion. Be creative: try putting the granola into glass canning jars and top them with either an attractive label or the back of recycled brown paper bags, tied in place with raffia ribbon.

2 cups old fashion rolled oats
1¼ cups sliced almonds
¾ cup sweetened flaked coconut
⅛ teaspoon salt
¼ cup vegetable oil
¼ cup honey
½ cup dried blueberries
½ cup dried cranberries
½ cup golden raisins or another dried fruit

Place oven rack to the middle position in your stove and preheat to 375°F.

Line a shallow baking tray with foil, brushed with oil, or use parchment paper.

Toss together oats, almonds, coconut, and salt in a large bowl.

Whisk together oil and honey well in a separate large bowl, and then stir in the oat mixture until well coated.

Spread mixture on the baking tray and bake, stirring occasionally until golden brown (25 to 30 minutes).

Stir in all the dried fruit, and then cool completely in the tray on a rack.

Swiss Chard, Leek & Gruyere Quiche

Chef Tricia Wheeler *(Columbus, OH)*

> Quiche was one of my family's favorite dinners and a frequent brunch meal on the weekends. My mother always had the ingredients on hand to make wonderful seasonal quiches. This is one that I like to make today in my own home.

12 ounces pâté brisée crust (see below)
1 leek, washed well and sliced into thin rings, white and pale green parts
1 pound Swiss chard, stems removed
2-4 tablespoons butter
3 eggs
1½ cups whole milk
3 ounces gruyere cheese, grated
Salt and freshly ground pepper

Pâté Brisée (based on classic French Shortcrust Pastry)
1¼ cups flour
½ teaspoon salt
½ cup unsalted butter cut into small pieces
5 tablespoons ice water

Pâté Brisée

In a large bowl, sift together flour and salt. Add the butter and rub in using your fingertips until fine crumbs form. Alternatively, you can use a food processor.

Slowly add the water, mixing until a crumbly dough begins to form (do not overwork dough). Pinch a piece; it should hold together. If the dough is crumbly, add a little more water. If it is wet and sticky, add a little flour.

Push the dough with one hand away from you until the dough is smooth and pliable. Flatten the dough to a round disc, and cover in plastic wrap. Chill for 2 hours or overnight. Leave to soften for 10 minutes at room temperature before rolling out.

Lightly butter a 9 to 10 inch quiche pan. On a lightly floured surface, roll out the dough to a thickness of ⅛-inch. Gently roll the
pastry around the rolling pin, and then unroll over the quiche pan,
leaving one in overhang.

With floured fingers, press the overhang down slightly toward the
base of the pan to reinforce the side. Then roll the rolling pan over
the rim to cut off the excess. Prick the base with a fork and chill for
1 hour.

Quiche

Preheat the oven to 400°F. Line the base of the crust with foil, add
baking beans, and bake for 15 minutes. Remove the foil and the
beans.

Reduce the oven's temperature to 350°F.

In a sauté pan, add 2 tablespoons of butter, and sauté leeks until
soft. In a separate pan, add 2 tablespoons of water and Swiss chard,
and sprinkle with salt and pepper. Put a lid on the pan until Swiss
chard is soft.

Reserve the Swiss chard and leeks. Beat together the eggs and milk,
and season with salt and pepper.

Sprinkle crust with gruyere, and spread the Swiss chard and leeks
over the cheese. Pour over the egg mixture, and bake for 35 to 45
minutes until set. Let cool slightly before slicing. Serve warm.

Sausage and Egg Strata

Mary Elizabeth

> Green peppers are always abundant in early fall. To take advantage of this colorful harvest, I have succeeded in finding ways to incorporate them into every course, including brunch, my favorite meal to host. Here is a recipe that can be prepared the night before and put in the oven just before your guests arrive.

4 cups whole milk
8 large eggs
2 teaspoons dry mustard powder
2 teaspoons salt
8 slices white bakery bread
(discard crust and cut bread into 1-inch cubes)
2 cups breakfast sausage, cooked and crumbled
(see recipe on page 21), or prepared sausage or diced ham
1 large green pepper, chopped
one small onion, chopped
1 cup cheddar cheese, grated

Butter a 9 x 12-inch glass baking dish.

In a large bowl, whisk eggs with milk, dry mustard, and salt to blend. Mix in the bread, sausage, green pepper, and onion. Mix thoroughly until the bread is moistened.

Transfer to the prepared dish. Cover and refrigerate overnight.

Bring to room temperature while you preheat the oven to 375 °F. Bake strata uncovered until just set in center (about 50 minutes). Sprinkle with cheese.

Bake until cheese melts (about 5 minutes). Let stand for 10 minutes and serve.

Homemade Breakfast Sausage

Chef Adam Goldgell *(Huntington, NY)*

15 pounds boned pork butts (ask butcher to grind)
8 tablespoons kosher salt
3 teaspoons ground white pepper
2 tablespoons onion powder
3 tablespoons garlic powder
3 tablespoons rubbed sage
1 ½ teaspoons ginger
1 tablespoon chili paste
5 teaspoons nutmeg
5 teaspoons thyme
2 ½ teaspoons cayenne pepper
3 cups ice water

Refrigerate ground pork until well chilled.

Thoroughly mix the remaining ingredients in a bowl.

Add them to the meat and mix.

Make the sausages into patties and use immediately, or cover each individually in clear plastic wrap to be refrigerated or frozen for later use.

Heat large skillet (a cast iron skillet is preferable) on high heat.

Add 1 tablespoon of blended oil (see Chef's Tips) to evenly coat the bottom of the skillet.

Gently drop patties in to allow to brown (approximately 5 minutes on each side). Then place in oven at 350°F until fully cooked.

Harvest Muffins

Monica

Fresh cranberries are plentiful in the fall between September and October. In anticipation of the coming holiday season, I buy bags of the fresh berry (produced mainly in New Jersey, Massachusetts, and Wisconsin), and refrigerate them by the bag. They last for a couple of months, and lend an interesting flavor to any meal. Combined with my blueberries (harvested in August, and then frozen), they make a pretty muffin top, and their round, firm texture makes each bite burst with flavor.

1 cup flour
⅓ cup sugar
1½ teaspoons baking powder
¼ teaspoon salt
¼ teaspoon ground nutmeg
¼ teaspoon salt
1 egg
⅓ cup milk
3 teaspoons extra virgin olive oil

½ teaspoon vanilla
½ cup blueberries
½ cup cranberries
½ cup chopped walnuts
½ cup chopped pecans
Cooking spray

Combine the dry ingredients. Combine the egg, milk, oil, and vanilla. Fold in three-quarters of the nuts.

Mix everything together gently with a wooden spoon (do not over mix).

Grease or place paper liners in tin. Spray a bit of cooking spray on the top of the muffin tin. Overfill with mixture (a little over three-quarters, almost to the top).

Mix the remaining nuts and fruit together and place on top of each muffin.

Bake at 375°F for 25 minutes or until a toothpick comes out clean

Cool for 10 minutes: 5 in tin and 5 on wire rack.

Breakfast Bread Pudding

Chef Geraldine Pollock *(Islip, NY)*

1 quart milk
18 ounces eggs, liquid
6 ounces sugar
1 teaspoon vanilla extract
1½ pounds leftover muffins (or crumbcake)
6 ounces butter, melted
4 ounces cranberries, dried

Cut bread into cubes and drizzle with melted butter.

Lay out on a sheet pan, bake at 325°F until toasted, let cool, and mix with cranberries.

In stainless steel bowl, combine eggs, milk, sugar, and vanilla, and mix well.

Pour custard over the bread and dried cranberries, and place into a buttered shallow baking dish.

Bake in water bath at 325°F for 40 minutes or until custard is set.

Serve warm or refrigerate for use later.

Part II

LUNCH:
SOUPS, SALADS & SANDWICHES

LUNCH:
SOUPS, SALADS & SANDWICHES

Unfortunately for many of us, lunch has become the "forgotten meal." This is the meal that often gets pushed aside because we are too busy. For some kids, it is traded away at school for a friend's cookies, and for us adults, it is often eaten on the go as we run from one meeting to the next.

Taking the time to stop for lunch can be just the midday respite that makes a busy schedule more bearable. You can meet with friends for lunch to chat, laugh, and take a break from a trying schedule, or simply stop to sit alone with a hot cup of soup. After some time to reflect and recoup, we can take on the rest of the day, feeling rejuvenated.

Lunch is also a great time to get your daily required vitamins and food groups. Munching on salads filled with garden vegetables such as ruby red beets, crisp orange carrots, and delicate green sprouts, topped with homemade dressing, contributes to an overall healthier you. Overstuffed sandwiches and soup can reach new heights when you fuse different flavors from around the world—curried chicken salad coupled with tomato soup or fragrant taboulleh with roasted red pepper hummus on whole wheat pita bread are just a couple of ways to transport your palette to other lands. When prepared with love the night before, there is something wonderful about taking your lunch to work or school. You know how good it is going to be, so you may look forward to your meal all morning. Exchanging recipes with your co-workers and sampling each other's creations, simple or sublime, can also be great fun.

Lunch is a simple pleasure to look forward to each day. Whether you are "brown bagging" it or dressed for success to meet up with your "lunch bunch," never forget the importance of having lunch. Including lunch as one of your several small meals throughout the day will not only improve your body's overall metabolism, but will also make your taste buds very happy and give you the boost and spring in your step that you need to wrap up your day.

Roasted Red Pepper and Goat Cheese Crostini

Chef Ashton Colleen Keefe *(New York, NY)*

> This recipe came from my mother's red pepper experiments in the kitchen. It can be made with basically everything and anything picked right from your garden in September. Our family variations include bleu cheese instead of goat (I recommend sticking with soft cheeses, though, because they melt and spread), onions, or sun-dried tomatoes—the sky is the limit. It is so simple and clean. Tasty without being pompous, this sandwich is the perfect way to get family and friends into the kitchen. Believe me, the crostini will be gone before you know it.

1 French baguette
4 roasted red peppers, diced, or 1 jar
2 cloves garlic, whole
Olive oil
Balsamic vinegar
1 long log goat cheese, room temperature
1 yellow onion, caramelized (optional)
3-5 pieces pancetta (or bacon), crisply cooked
Salt and pepper to taste

Take a French baguette and slice it once across its equator.

With the oven on broil, place the two pieces of the baguette under the broiler until they begin to toast. Pull them out and rub with a clove of garlic (one per side).

While the bread is still warm, spread room-temperature goat cheese onto both sides, top with roasted red peppers, onion, crisply cooked pancetta (or bacon), and place back under the broiler until the cheese begins to bubble.

Remove from the oven and drizzle reduced balsamic vinegar (or nice aged balsamic) over the baguettes and cut. Serve warm.

How to Make Crostini

Take one loaf of a thin baguette, cut the bread as thin as you can, and brush with blended oil (see Chef's Tips). Toast until hard to the touch.

How to Caramelize Onions

Heat pan on high. Add 1 teaspoon of vegetable oil and 2 table-spoons of butter to evenly coat the bottom of the pan, and add your cut-up yellow onions. Spread out the onion evenly to cover the surface area of the pan. When you add the onion, you must hear a sizzling sound, which means the pan is hot enough (use a pan large enough, so, it evenly coats the surface area). Wait until the natural sugars in the onion come to the surface, and look for the beautiful caramel color. Then give it a good stir until you have achieved the dark brown color throughout. Add ½ cup of white wine to deglaze the pan. Turn the temperature to low, and allow the wine to reduce and the onions to soften.

Curried Chicken Salad

Monica

> I experiment by using Indian curry powder in just about everything, even oatmeal (for oatmeal, try using a sprinkle each of cinnamon and curry powder, yellow raisins, a drop of maple syrup, and a dot of butter). Invigorate chicken salad by using curry. The combination is so rich and satisfying, and the yellow, green, and red colors seem to jump off the plate. Use more curry if you like your food spicier. The warmth generated from the curry is a welcome touch on a chilly autumn afternoon.

2 chicken breasts, baked and shredded
2-3 tablespoons mayonnaise
1-2 tablespoons Indian curry powder
⅛ cup slivered almonds
¼ cup red and green grapes sliced in half
3 scallions sliced thin, green left on
1 teaspoon apple cider vinegar

Bake chicken breasts, debone, and shred (or use leftover roast chicken).

Mix together curry and mayonnaise, and then mix with chicken.

Add the almonds, grapes, scallions, and vinegar.

Serve on a bed of lettuce or whole grain bread.

Taboulleh

Monica

Taboulleh is a quick and healthy way to bring your green herbs straight from the kitchen garden to your table. This is a Middle Eastern dish that I learned from the Atlantic Avenue chefs in Brooklyn Heights. It complements any meat entrée or can stand alone, accompanied by fresh, smoked red pepper hummus and whole wheat pita chips.

3 tablespoons bulghur wheat
½ medium onion, chopped
1 teaspoon salt
½ teaspoon allspice
1 pound medium tomatoes, finely chopped
3 cups flat leaf parsley, minced
½ cup mint leaves, chopped fine
⅛ cup extra virgin olive oil
Juice of 1 large lemon

Prepare the bulghur, softening in warm water for 10 minutes. Drain and set aside.

Mix onion with the salt and allspice.

Combine bulghur, onion, tomatoes, parsley, mint, oil, and lemon juice in a large bowl.

Refrigerate until ready to serve.

There are several combinations of basic herbs and spices harvested in the fall that are specific to certain international cuisine. Here are just a few highlights that can turn any dish into something far more exciting in minutes:

Greek: cloves, Greek oregano, mint, parsley; **Indian:** curry, turmeric, coriander, cardamom; **Mexican:** chili powder, cumin, cilantro; **Chinese:** ginger, garlic, scallions; **Middle Eastern:** allspice and nutmeg.

Roasted Red Pepper Hummus

Mary Elizabeth

> I like to add different flavors such as finely chopped roasted red pepper to my basic hummus recipe to change it up. Peppers are always plentiful at my house in September, even though I only plant one pack of peppers in my garden each year.

4 cups garbanzos (chickpeas), reserve liquid
½ cup tahini (sesame paste)
⅓ cup reserved liquid
⅓ cup olive oil
Juice of 2 or 3 lemons
4 cloves garlic, minced
1½ teaspoons salt
2 teaspoons ground cumin
Paprika, for garnish
Freshly ground black pepper to taste
Roasted red peppers to taste (optional)

Combine chickpeas, tahini, reserved liquid, olive oil, and the juice of 1 lemon in the bowl of the food processor, fitted with a steel blade. Process until smooth and creamy, pausing once or twice to scrape down the sides of the bowl with a spatula (consistency will be similar to peanut butter).

Add the garlic, salt, cumin, roasted red pepper, and black pepper to taste. Blend in the food processor. Add more lemon juice or another clove of garlic to taste.

Lettuce Boats Filled with Corn Salsa

1 (19 ounce) can black beans, rinsed and drained
1 (19 ounce) can corn, drained or fresh corn
½ red bell pepper, chopped
1 bunch scallions, chopped
½ bunch cilantro, chopped
Juice from 1 lime
2 teaspoons olive oil
1 teaspoon ground cumin
1 clove garlic, chopped
½ teaspoon salt
2 rings jalapeño peppers, chopped
1 head Boston lettuce

Mix all ingredients in a bowl.

Refrigerate until serving.

Take a lettuce leaf and fill with salsa.

Chicken and Bean Burritos

Chef Adam Goldgell *(Huntington, NY)*

Chicken

1 whole chicken

4 cups chicken stock

2 cans chipotle in adobe

Rice

¾ cup cooked wild rice

2⅓ cups water

1 teaspoon kosher salt

Salsa

1 red pepper, minced

1 green pepper, minced

2 ripe medium tomatoes or 4 plum tomatoes, cored and diced

2 avocados, halved, seeded, and diced

½ medium yellow onion, finely diced

2 jalapeños, seeded, stemmed, and minced

½ cup fresh cilantro leaves, chopped

1 teaspoon kosher salt

Beans

2 tablespoons cumin

3 tablespoons extra virgin olive oil

½ medium onion, finely chopped

½ medium red and green peppers

3 cloves garlic, minced

Kosher salt

1 (19 ounce) can pinto beans, rinsed and drained

2 cups smoked gouda, shredded

4 extra large (12-inch) whole flour tortillas (or whole wheat)

Sour cream and lime wedges for garnish

Chicken

Cook the chicken in chicken stock and chipotle, and then pick off all the meat and remove the bones. Once the chicken is cooked, reduce liquid by half.

Rice

Bring the water to a boil over high heat in a medium saucepan with a tightly fitting lid. Stir in rice and salt. Simmer gently for over 30 to 35 minutes. Remove from the heat and let it stand covered for 10 minutes. Fluff with a fork.

Salsa

Mix all ingredients in a bowl and set aside.

Beans

Heat olive oil in a medium skillet over medium heat. Add the onions and red and green peppers until slightly soft. Add garlic and season with ½ teaspoon of salt and cumin.

Add the beans and mash them until the mixture is almost smooth. Set aside.

Assembling the Burritos

When ready to assemble, heat the burritos. Wrap in a slightly damp towel and microwave for about 1 to 2 minutes until pliable. Spoon about a quarter of both rice and beans, ¾ cup of salsa, ½ cup of cheese, and ½ cup of chicken into the center of a tortilla. Fold in the sides and roll the tortilla away from you to form a package.

Serve with sour cream, lime, and remaining salsa.

Backyard Grape Jam

Monica

Here is a new take on the classic lunchbox favorite, peanut butter and jelly. I prefer jam over jelly. Making your own grape jam from your backyard fruit results in the epitome of taste and freshness: garden to table. Don't grow grapes in your garden? Visit a local orchard or winery that does, and pick your own in the fall. Take a trip to historic Concord, MA, the home of Concord grapes (the easiest to skin), and pick coolers-full to bring home. Your local market has an abundance of grapes. If Concord is not available, red grapes are extremely sweet and satisfying for a lighter jam. This is easily refrigerated for 2 to 3 weeks; frozen for up to a year.

8 cups grapes, skins and pulp separated
6 cups sugar

Skin the grapes by holding the ripe grape between your fingers and squeezing to pop out the pulp, and set the pulp aside. Boil the skins in ⅛ cup of water for about 10 minutes or until almost all the water has boiled off. Boil the grape pulp, barely covering with water for about 10 minutes, stirring, and then press through a strainer to remove the seeds. Combine the skins and pulp. Heat to your desired thickness, cool, and refrigerate or freeze in sterilized jars. Add a little lemon juice if you cannot achieve the thickness you are trying for. Adding lemon juice or vinegar also helps to preserve the jam longer.

Homemade Peanut Butter

Monica

> I am always trying to make what I buy from the market at home in my own kitchen so I can control the salt, sugar, and preservative levels in what I eat. Making your own golden nut butter is extremely satisfying. Use softer nuts like peanuts, cashews, or hazelnuts. If you are not a sandwich lover, use the peanut butter as a dip for apples.

3 pounds roasted peanuts, shelled and skinned
12 tablespoons extra virgin olive oil
Salt and sugar (or stevia) to taste

Shell and skin your roasted peanuts. Mix with the olive oil and pulverize until smooth in a food processor. If you would like it creamier, add more olive oil; crunchier, less oil and less pulverizing. Add in a miniscule amount of salt and sugar (or stevia) to flavor. It is not necessary to add anything. Serve your peanut butter and jelly on whole grain bread. Make it weekly in small batches for school lunches.

Spanakopita or Spinach Pie

(Pairs well with Greek Salad)

Chef Adam Goldgell *(Huntington, NY)*

2 tablespoons butter

⅓ cup olive oil or canola oil

2 pounds spinach, washed and drained

1 small bunch scallions, chopped (use both white and green parts)

⅓ cup parsley

¼ cup cilantro

½ cup red onion, chopped

½ pound feta cheese, crumbled

2 eggs

1 cup unsalted butter, melted

1 pound phyllo sheets

Salt and pepper to taste

Place butter in a sauté pan and add spinach. Cook until wilted.

Allow to cool and squeeze out all the liquids by hand. Then chop and set aside.

Place red onions and 2 tablespoons of scallions in a pan with some olive oil and a spoon of butter, sautéing for 3 to 4 minutes until clear.

Add parsley, cilantro, salt, and pepper to taste. Remove from the heat and cool.

Beat eggs in a separate bowl and add to the spinach mixture.

Stir in feta cheese and add the onion-scallion combination.

Follow the phyllo assembly steps below, and then bake for 45 minutes until golden brown on top. Let it stand for 15 minutes before eating.

Working with Phyllo Sheets

Don't be intimidated: once you have done it once, you realize that it is not hard, and you will appreciate the rewards of biting into a flaky, buttery pastry. The most important tip is not to let the phyllo sheets dry out. Consequently, you must work very quickly. Phyllo dough should be kept refrigerated. Take out of the refrigerator, and set on your counter to bring it to room temperature just before you start to prepare the filling.

In order to make sure the strips do not dry out, you must have your filling completely ready before you start working with the phyllo sheets. You should also leave them in their plastic bag until you are ready to start the assembly process. Then take 2 cotton towels and place them under water, ringing out well. When you have opened and taken the sheets out of the plastic bag, cover them with one of the damp cloths. Brush the bottom of a jelly roll pan, slowly unfold, and place one full sheet in the pan. They are paper-thin and very delicate, so you must gently and lightly brush each sheet using a pastry brush dipped in melted butter. Continue to repeat the process 3 times quickly (using a total of 4 sheets).

Place your mixture on top and cover with another sheet. Bake as directed above.

As an alternative to a traditional apple pie, you can use the apple pie filling found on page 124 (see Apple Pie), and make an apple strudel by altering the technique slightly. Rather than placing your first sheet in a jelly roll pan, place it on a damp cloth on your work surface, and lay out one sheet at a time (for a total of 4). After brushing each sheet with the melted butter, however, sprinkle lightly with a mixture of finely ground nuts and sugar or pound cake crumbs. Place all the filling close to one end in a mound, take the edge of the towel on that end, and slowly start to roll it up. Place the seam side down on your baking sheet and bake at 350 °F for 30 minutes.

Greek Salad

Jane Suhr *(Blue Point, NY)*

(Pairs well with Spinach Pie)

<u>Serves 8</u>

Salad

5 cups torn green and red lettuce

1 tomato, coarsely chopped

½ cup cucumber, sliced

1 red onion, thinly sliced

1 can black olives, drained and sliced

1 cup feta cheese, chopped

Dressing

⅓ cup olive oil

3 tablespoons red wine vinegar

2 tablespoons freshly squeezed lemon juice

½ teaspoon dried oregano

1 teaspoon sugar

1 clove garlic, minced

¼ teaspoon pepper

2-4 tablespoons fresh dill, chopped

Mix the salad ingredients in a bowl.

Prepare the dressing by mixing all the ingredients in a screw-top jar and shake.

Add the dressing and croutons immediately prior to serving.

Lobster Salad on Garlic Crostini with Mango Salsa

Chef Adam Goldgell *(Huntington, NY)*

> Fresh herbs and vegetables like cilantro, chives, and peppers, still plentiful in your garden come September, can be used in this dish. It is especially welcoming on a late summer day in the fall, when you are seeking a "cool" lunch or dinner to make.

Lobster Salad

1 pound cooked lobster meat
¼ cup mayonnaise
Zest and juice from one lemon (keep separate)
¼ cup chives, finely chopped
1 red pepper, diced
1 small red onion, diced
1 tablespoon each garlic and onion powder

Mango Salsa

1 whole mango, peeled and finely chopped
¼ cup chopped cilantro
3 tablespoons rice vinegar
Pinch of cayenne pepper
Salt and black pepper to taste

Lobster Salad

Combine all ingredients and set aside.

Mango Salsa

Combine all ingredients and set aside.

Serve lobster salad with crostini (see page 29) and topped with a small amount of salsa.

Chai Lentil Salad

Nini Ordoubadi *(Andes, NY)*

Tea is not only a refreshing, delicious, and healthy beverage, but also one of the most versatile and interesting ingredients that is (finally) hitting the Western culinary scene. I recommend that you experiment with using your favorite teas in your culinary exploration. This spicy chai lentil salad is perfect for fall. Just as many chefs say of cooking with wine, "do not cook with a wine that you wouldn't drink," for the best results, use the best-quality loose leaf teas that you can get your hands on—not grocery store tea bags. Buy your teas directly from tea purveyors and blenders who carry only high-quality loose leaf teas that are fresh and flavorful, and cut your herbs directly from your garden.

2 cups French lentils
3 cups chai tea, brewed strong
4 cloves garlic
1 medium onion
3 tablespoons olive oil
1 cup fresh cilantro
½ cup fresh mint
½ cup fresh basil
Sea salt to taste

Cook lentils in tea until done (about 30 minutes).

Sauté garlic and onion in 3 tablespoons of olive oil.

Toss in the fresh herbs.

Add to lentils and season with sea salt to taste.

Bibb Salad with Sage Vinaigrette

Chef Heather Merriken *(Camden, ME)*

Whenever the leaves start to change, I think of apples, sage, and all the beautiful pumpkins and squashes that the fall season brings. In my native New Jersey, we love to go apple and pumpkin picking, and then bring our goods home to make baked apples, pies, and roasted squash. I always use fresh herbs to complement the robust, vivid flavors of the season.

2 heads Bibb lettuce
1 small butternut squash, diced into ½-inch cubes
1 tablespoon plus 2 teaspoons finely chopped fresh sage
1 tablespoon plus ¼ cup good quality olive oil
2 tablespoons vegetable oil
1 McIntosh apple, unpeeled
1 Golden Delicious apple, peeled
1 teaspoon whole grain mustard
Juice of 1 lemon

1 tablespoon hazelnut or walnut oil
1 garlic clove, peeled and smashed
1 teaspoon fresh thyme
Kosher salt and freshly ground pepper to taste

Preheat oven to 450°F. In a medium bowl, toss cubed butternut squash with 1 tablespoon of olive oil and 2 tablespoons of vegetable oil until just coated. Sprinkle 1 tablespoon of the chopped sage leaves over the squash, and season liberally with salt and pepper. Spread the squash out on a cookie sheet and place in a preheated oven for 30 minutes. Turn the squash with a spatula every 10 minutes to ensure even cooking.

Meanwhile, prepare sage vinaigrette by combining mustard, lemon juice, ½ teaspoon of salt, and 1 teaspoon of freshly ground black pepper in a small bowl, and whisk to combine. Then slowly drizzle ¼ cup of olive oil into the bowl, tablespoon by tablespoon, whisking steadily until emulsified.

Next, whisk in the hazelnut oil. Add the garlic clove, thyme, and remaining sage and stir. Mandolin or very thinly slice both apples directly into the vinaigrette. Evenly coat apple slices with dressing to prevent browning. Clean Bibb lettuce leaves and dry thoroughly. Remove the butternut cubes from the oven and set aside to cool. To assemble the salad, place Bibb leaves in a large bowl. Season lightly with salt and pepper. Then add macerated apples slices, squash, and a tablespoon of dressing. Toss. Taste and adjust seasoning and the amount of dressing accordingly.

Autumn Squash Salad

Chef Meredith Machemer *(Grey Horse Tavern, Bayport, NY)*

> This recipe was developed in keeping with our philosophy, "No Farms, No Food," and our menu reflects our support of local farms, sustainable fisheries, and humanely raised meats and dairy items. The squash, apples, and mache are locally picked from a farm on Long Island in late September-early October.

Vinaigrette
½ cup Spanish olive oil
½ cup sunflower oil or grapeseed oil
½ cup champagne vinegar or apple cider vinegar
¼ cup good quality honey (local honey is best)
Kosher salt and fresh ground pepper to taste

Salad
2 each medium-large butternut squash
4-5 McIntosh apples (core and slice at time of salad assembly)
3 cups mache rosettes (see box)
½ cup whole almonds, toasted and roughly chopped
½ cup good quality crumbled goat cheese

> Mache is a type of salad green that is available in many specialty grocery stores or at your local farm stand. It is also known as lamb's lettuce, corn salad, field salad, or field lettuce. Mache grows in rosettes or loose bunches.

Preheat oven to 400°F.

Vinaigrette

In a medium mixing bowl, combine vinegar and honey, and whisk until completely combined.

Gradually whisk in the oils and season to taste with kosher salt and fresh ground pepper. Set aside.

Salad

Line a rimmed baking sheet with parchment paper and set aside.

Peel and seed squash and cut into 1-inch cubes.

Place diced squash in a large bowl, drizzle with olive oil, and season with kosher salt and fresh ground pepper. Toss to coat.

Spread the squash evenly onto the parchment-lined baking sheet.

Roast in the 400°F oven for 35 to 45 minutes (you want the squash to have some bite to it; you do not want it to be mushy). Once finished, set aside to cool.

Lay out the almonds onto a parchment-lined baking sheet. Toast in the oven for 6 to 7 minutes (you will start to smell the aroma of the almonds when finished).

Let the almonds cool and then roughly chop. Set aside.

In a large mixing bowl, add mache rosettes, roasted squash, and apple slices.

Season with 1 teaspoon of kosher salt and ¼ tsp of fresh black pepper.

Dress with ¼ to ½ cup of vinaigrette and toss to coat.

Serve onto individual salad plates, making sure to evenly distribute apples, mache, and squash.

Sprinkle each salad with crumbled goat cheese and toasted almonds.

Caesar Salad

Kate Saggio *(Vineland, NJ)*

> Growing up on a produce farm in southern New Jersey always brings to mind such wonderful memories. Along with the memories comes the deep appreciation for fresh seasonal lettuces and salad recipes. The fall variations of romaine and spinach are my favorite. The following recipe is from the kitchen of my father, who prepares it as his parents and grandparents had for many years on the same farm. It is now a favorite of my entire family. He does not use a recipe, so these are "guesstimates;" feel free to "play" with them.

1 head romaine lettuce, torn into bite-size pieces
1 can "flat" anchovy filets (optional)
1-3 cloves of garlic, minced
1 egg yolk
1 cup olive oil
2 tablespoons lemon juice, freshly squeezed
¾ cup romano cheese
Black olives and croutons (optional)

Mix in the anchovy filets, garlic, and egg in a blender to a paste-like consistency. While still mixing in the blender, drizzle in the olive oil and lemon juice. Place the dressing in a jar or container with a tight lid (for shaking).

Add romano cheese and freshly ground pepper to taste, and shake until well blended. Drizzle over fresh romaine, and garnish with black olives and croutons.

In place of a raw egg, try substituting a soft-boiled egg (boil for approximately 3 minutes), using the liquidy yolk center.

Grilled chicken or shrimp are always a nice addition to make your Caesar salad a complete meal.

Toss your Caesar salad immediately before serving.

Spinach Salad

½ cup olive oil
½ cup red wine vinegar
¼ cup chopped onions
¼ cup sugar
1 ½ teaspoons paprika
1 teaspoon dry mustard powder
1 teaspoon salt
½ teaspoon black pepper
10 ounces baby spinach
4 slices crisply cooked bacon, broken into bits
2 hard-boiled eggs, chopped

Mix all the dressing in a jar and shake.

Assemble the salad in a bowl. Toss with salad dressing immediately before serving.

Minestrone Soup
(a.k.a. Witches Brew)

Diane Nedelkoff *(Ramsey, NJ)*

Every Halloween, all of my family comes to my house for trick-or-treating because our streets are close together and the kids can get lots of candy in a short time. They all look forward to my cauldron of minestrone soup. The kids call it my "Witches Brew," and it is always hot and ready for anyone that comes through the door that night. I serve it with a tossed salad and hot crusty rolls. It is the perfect thing for a chilly October night.

1 pound bacon
1 onion, chopped
2 cloves minced garlic
1 (28 ounce) can crushed tomatoes
2 quarts chicken broth
1 cubed turnip, potato, and parsnip
2 chopped celery stalks
2 chopped carrots
Finely chopped parsley
1 can drained kidney beans
1 box frozen peas
½ pound cooked pasta, shells
Salt and pepper to taste

Brown 1 pound of bacon in a soup pot until crisp. Remove bacon from the pot and set aside. Pour out all but 2 tablespoons of bacon fat.

Sauté onion and garlic cloves until lightly brown. Add the rest of the ingredients.

Cook for approximately 2 hours.

When ready to eat, add the cooked pasta, kidney beans, and frozen peas.

Cook for an additional 1/2 hour on low heat.

Serve with leftover crumbled bacon bits and grated cheese.

Pumpkin Bisque

Chef Maureen Denning *(Snapper Inn, Oakdale, NY)*

> Pumpkins are harvested in October and are a substantial staple in soups, casseroles, and desserts—and, of course, are also popular for decorating.

2 ounces oil
¼ pound butter (1 tablespoon reserved for roasted pumpkin)
1 bunch celery, leaves and hearts removed, roughly chopped
3 large white onions, roughly chopped
1 large pumpkin, peeled, seeded, cut into 2-3-inch cubes, and roasted
½ cups brown sugar
1 quart chicken stock (1 cup reserved for roasted pumpkin)
2 quarts heavy cream
2 tablespoons cinnamon
2 teaspoons ground cloves
Salt and pepper to taste

Heat oil and butter. Sauté celery and onion until clear (on medium heat).

Add brown sugar, and stir until melted.

Add pumpkin and chicken stock, and bring to a boil. Strain through sieve.

Add to the cream, and stir frequently.

Season with cinnamon, salt, and pepper. Slowly reboil and serve.

How to Roast Pumpkin

Spread pumpkin cubes onto baking sheet and spread into one even layer.

Roast in the oven for at least 1 hour until they are fork tender and crispy on the outside. To ensure even browning, use a metal spatula to flip cubes during roasting.

Tomato Basil Soup

Mary Kay Ratigan *(Huntington, CT)*

<u>Serves 4</u>

We typically plant more than we need, so we are always looking for ways to use all those tomatoes and basil from our gardens in September. This soup is a perfect way to finish them. You can also jar the rest of the tomatoes to have throughout the winter.

1 large red onion, chopped
1 tablespoon butter
1 tablespoon ginger, minced
1 tablespoon brown sugar
4 cups whole Roma or plum tomatoes, diced
5 cups chicken stock
1 cup basil leaves
Salt and pepper to taste (freshly cracked pepper always adds more flavor)

In a large saucepan, caramelize the onions in butter, ginger, and sugar. Add the tomatoes and bring to a simmer. Season with salt and pepper

Add the stock and simmer on low heat until very soft (at least 20 minutes). Add the basil and puree.

Cook on low heat for 40 minutes.

How to Peel a Tomato

An easy way to loosen the skins from tomatoes is to blanch them. To do this, core a few tomatoes, and then place them in a pot of boiling water until the skins start to split. Immediately remove them from the water and place them in a bowl of iced water. With a sharp knife, start on the top edge and begin to peel.

Onion Soup

Lorraine Ott *(Boxford, MA)*

> Early in the fall, as the temperature starts to drop and a chill is in the air, my family will ask me to make my onion soup. It makes a hearty and filling lunch.

3 tablespoons butter
4 tablespoons olive oil
6 pounds onions, sliced and chopped
2 garlic cloves, minced
¾ teaspoon sugar
4½ tablespoons flour
12 cups beef stock
2-3 dashes Tabasco sauce
1 package mozzarella

Melt butter and oil. Add onions and garlic and cook until soft for 30 minutes.

Add sugar and cook for an additional 45 minutes until the onions are a deep golden brown.

Add flour, beef stock, and Tabasco sauce, and bring to a boil. Then simmer for 45 minutes.

Serve in a bowl with a slice of French bread topped with a piece of mozzarella. Broil briefly until the cheese is bubbly and melted.

Split Pea Soup

Chef Adam Goldgell *(Huntington, NY)*

> When I think of comfort foods, homemade split pea soup is one that comes to mind. It is a good way to take the chill off as the temperature starts to cool down.

1 cup salted pork, divided into 2 equal chunks (or bacon)
3 carrots, chopped
1 cup Spanish onions, finely chopped
4 cloves garlic, minced
1 tablespoon fresh oregano, chopped (or 1 teaspoon dried oregano)
1 teaspoon chili powder
1 tablespoon black pepper
1 tablespoon kosher salt
2 cups potatoes, diced
1½ cups dried split peas
14 cups chicken stock
⅛ cup olive oil
⅛ cup parsley, chopped
3 yellow onions, quartered
¼ cup white wine

Sauté onions and garlic in olive oil until translucent in a pot large enough to accommodate the stock.

Add oregano, salt, and pepper, mixing, again, until the onions become translucent.

Add carrots, cooking the carrots for 2 to 3 minutes.

Put the salt pork and wine in with the onion mixture. Deglaze the bottom of the pan by making sure everything is taken up.

Pour the split peas and the potatoes on top, and then pour the stock in.

Keep stirring and cooking over medium heat for 45 minutes until the peas are starting to fall apart.

Depending on the desired consistency, you can puree half of it and pour it back into the pot, or puree the entire amount.

Curried Butternut Squash Soup

Chef Nicole Roarke *(Blue Point, NY)*

> The day my Mom first made her curried butternut squash soup, it became infamous in our household. From that day on, there has never been a special fall dinner that did not include this soup. I have since changed the recipe a bit to make it my own. Once you have prepared the squash, the remaining steps are quite easy to follow, and the end result will have your guests requesting it for many dinners to come.

4 cups butternut squash cubes or 2 (16 ounce) cans puréed butternut squash
1 stick butter
2 tablespoons blended oil
6 cups chicken stock
2 cups heavy cream
2 large yellow onions, diced
2 tablespoons curry (powdered, yellow)
3 tablespoons sugar
4 Granny Smith apples, diced
1 cup apple cider
½ cup roasted garlic gloves
Salt and pepper to taste

In a large pot, sweat the onions in butter and oil. Once the onions are translucent and soft, add the roasted garlic. Stir in the butternut squash and apples. Be sure to coat each piece with the onion mixture.

Add the stock and cider and bring to a boil, then lowering to a simmer. Simmer over a low heat for at least 30 minutes until the squash is tender when pierced with a fork. Stir carefully to make sure nothing is stuck to the bottom of the pot. Using a blender, food processor, or hand-held mixer, puree the soup.

Add the cream, sugar, curry, salt, and pepper to taste. If the soup is too thick, add more chicken stock, ½ cup at a time until the desired consistency is reached.

Garnish before serving with fresh dill sprigs or flat-leaf Italian parsley.

Preparing Butternut Squash

Squash can be found in a can or even frozen in chunks. It can be intimidating and time consuming to hack away at the oversized orange gourd for 4 cups of this delicious ingredient, but my family and I always use the real thing. After years of making this soup, we have perfected the preparation of this vegetable.

We have found that the easiest and most efficient way to prepare butternut squash is to use a potato peeler with a horizontal blade. Hold the squash in your hand, and simply peel from stem to root, removing all the outside skin and any white layers until you have reached the orange meaty flesh.

Butternut squash is in season during the fall when the gourd itself is large and the flesh is bright to deep orange. If it is light in color, it is not fully ripe, and using canned puree would be best.

Pumpkin Ravioli with Butter and Sage

Chef Roland A. Iadanza *(West Babylon, NY)*

Serves 4

> The chill of fall gets us in the mood for earthy, stick-to-ribs, comfort-type foods. This is a delectable dish that, at first glance, can be perceived as too heavy, so I like to serve it at brunch, when you can have a taste along with other lighter fare.

24 large, round pumpkin ravioli
8 tablespoons unsalted butter
8 fresh sage leaves, chopped and whole
1 large amaretti cookie
2 tablespoons salt
4 ounces grated parmigiano-reggiano cheese

Bring 6 quarts of water to a boil and add 2 tablespoons of salt. Drop ravioli in the boiling water and gently stir, cooking for 3 to 5 minutes. While the pasta is cooking, melt the butter in a large sauté pan until it foams and subsides. Add 4 tablespoons of pasta to the boiling water and whisk to emulsify. Drain ravioli and add to the butter. Add the sage leaves and toss gently for 1 minute over medium heat to coat the ravioli with sauce. Place 6 ravioli on 4 warmed plates, grate the parmigiano-reggiano cheese and amaretti cookie over each plate, and serve immediately.

Autumn Squash Soup with Gruyere Cheese Gratin

Chef Roland A. Iadanza *(West Babylon, NY)*

6 acorn squash, equal in size, tops cut off and bottom trimmed so squash can stand up straight
4 tablespoons sweet butter
1 medium onion, chopped
1 leek chopped and washed well
2 cloves garlic, minced
1 celery root, peeled and cut into chunks
6 cups chicken stock (if canned, use low-sodium)
1 large or 2 small butternut squashes, peeled and cut into chunks
½ cup heavy cream
6 ¼-inch slices of baguette bread, brushed with butter and toasted
1 cup gruyere cheese, grated
Sachet of herbs: cheesecloth filled with thyme, rosemary, bay leaf, parsley, and basil, tied with string
½ cup sour cream, thinned with a little heavy cream and placed in squeeze bottle
Sugar, salt, and pepper to taste

In a large saucepan or casserole, heat butter over medium heat. Add onion, leek, and garlic, and cook for 30 minutes, stirring occasionally.

Add butternut squash, celery root, chicken stock, and sachet of herbs. Bring to a boil and simmer for 30 minutes or until very tender.

Remove sachet and discard. Puree soup with hand-held blender until smooth. Add cream and season, returning to a simmer for about 5 minutes.

Add soup to acorn squash shell and bake at 375°F for 30 minutes. Remove from the oven, place crouton on the soup and cheese, and place back in the oven for 10 more minutes until cheese is slightly brown and bubbling.

Serve on plate with dolly or in soup bowl.

Variations

A shortcut is to prebake the acorn shell, add the hot soup, crouton, and cheese, and bake off.

Serve soup in bowls and make a design with the sour cream in a squeeze bottle. Let your guests make their own designs.

Other ingredients to add are caraway seeds or curry when you are sautéing the onions and leeks. Apples may be added when the squash goes in.

Grandma Raymond's Spaetzle Soup

Annie Bailey *(Malverne, NY)*

<u>Makes 14 cups</u>

Whenever my grandmother would visit us, I always looked forward to the days when she would make her spaetzle soup, especially during Oktoberfest, when tomatoes were plentiful. My fondest memories include coming in from school to find the house filled with its delicious aroma. To this day, it is one of my favorite recipes. It is basically a beef and vegetable soup filled with an abundance of spaetzle. My grandma's spaetzle are a little different than other versions of this German noodle. They are irregular in shape and firm in texture, somewhere between a noodle and a dumpling. Like so many soups, this tastes even better the next day.

Soup

4 cups chicken broth

8 cups water

1½ pounds beef chuck, cut into 1-inch pieces

1 (28 ounce) can whole tomatoes in juice, chopped

3 stalks celery (with leaves), sliced

2 carrots, peeled and sliced

1 medium onion, diced

1 teaspoon salt

1 bay leaf

Spaetzle

1½ cups flour

2 large eggs

½ cup milk

½ teaspoon salt

Soup

Combine broth, water, and beef in a large pot. Bring to a boil over high heat.

Reduce heat, and let beef simmer for 45 minutes. Skim off foam, if any.

Add tomatoes and their juice, celery, carrots, onion, salt, and bay leaf. Let simmer for about 45 minutes or until the beef is tender.

Spaetzle

In a large bowl, combine flour, eggs, milk, and salt to make a sticky dough.

Turn dough out onto a dinner plate. Tilt the plate over the simmering soup. With a knife, cut thin strips of the dough from the edge of the plate and let the pieces drop into the soup. Dip the knife into the soup occasionally to prevent sticking. Don't worry about the size of the pieces: some will be bigger than others. Try to make them about the width of a pencil or slightly larger.

Let the spaetzle simmer in the soup for 20 minutes. Remove the bay leaf before serving.

Refrigerator Soup

Monica

In the fall months, my son requests a new soup each week as part of a tradition that started one very snowy Saturday afternoon many years ago when I did not want to go out to the store. Instead, I came up with leftover pot roast soup.

I now empty the fridge weekly and turn leftover vegetables, sauces, and meats into a wholesome, hot, and healthy meal to be enjoyed all weekend. If it turns out really good, I write it down and try to recreate it again. On busy weekends, I pop whatever is leftover into the freezer (no matter how small) for future use. Even just two slices of leftover spiral ham can be used to flavor pea soup or clam chowder. Each soup comes out differently because their outcome is fully determined by what is in the fridge and nearing the end of its shelf life. In this case, I had a lovely eggplant that was about to expire.

Extra virgin olive oil for sautéing
½ small eggplant with skin left on, cubed
1 small onion
Garlic powder, dried onion pieces, and dried parsley
1 cup celery diced
1 cup baby carrots
1 can kidney beans, drain liquid
3 large jarred roasted red peppers cut into strips
¾ cup small, whole, seedless black olives
1 small can tomato puree
1 (20 ounce) can diced tomatoes, flavored with basil, garlic, and oregano
1 cup grape tomatoes
3 cups hot water and an additional sprinkling of garlic powder, dried onion pieces, and parsley
Salt to taste

Sauté all the ingredients in the order written, softening the eggplant and spices a bit first, and then stirring in each new addition.

Once the water is added, simmer for 45 to 60 minutes, depending on how soft you like your veggies.

Serve small-shaped whole wheat pasta (like tubatini) in a large bowl, so, each person can control their own portion when adding to their soup.

If you are dieting, do not add the pasta. If you are in the mood for meat, add in one large, cooked, shredded chicken breast or crumbled pieces of leftover meatloaf (have them stored in your freezer, ready to use for times like these). Or, try adding a couple of handfuls of medium-frozen or cooked shrimp (tail on), and turn it into a seafood vegetable soup. I take all the tails off the shrimp before serving at the table. Add any of these additional ingredients to the soup for the last 10 to 15 minutes of cooking.

Moroccan Spiced Carrot Soup

Chef Heather Merriken *(Camden, ME)*

Nothing says "soul food" to me more than the earthy, exotic spices of the Middle East. In this recipe, I have utilized some of my favorite Moroccan flavors in an American classic. I often pick the spices from my garden, because the better the quality of your spices, the better this soup will be. If possible, find a Middle Eastern or Indian grocery in your neighborhood to buy imported loose spices. These tend to be fresher and have more zing than grocery varieties.

1 pound carrots
1 Yukon gold potato
1 small sweet potato
1 small yellow onion
1 small red onion
2 tablespoons ground turmeric
1 tablespoon ground cumin
2 tablespoons sweet paprika
1 tablespoon hot paprika
2 teaspoons ground dried ginger
2 teaspoons dried oregano
2 teaspoons red chili flake
1 teaspoon sugar
1 teaspoon ground cinnamon
Pinch (approximately ⅛ teaspoon) nutmeg
6 cups vegetable stock (see Chef's Tips)
1 (16 ounce) can unseasoned plum tomatoes, including juice
½ bunch parsley
½ cup good quality olive oil
Kosher salt and freshly ground pepper to taste

Preheat oven to 375°F.

In a small bowl, combine all spices with 2 tablespoons of kosher salt and 1 tablespoon of pepper.

Peel and chop carrots, potatoes, and onions into large chunks. Spread in an even layer onto two cookie sheets.

Drizzle ¼ cup of olive oil onto each sheet. Sprinkle herbs and mix over vegetables evenly. With a spoon (or hands), toss the vegetables with the olive oil and herbs to ensure proper coating.

Roast vegetables in the oven for 45 minutes to 1 hour until tender. Stir vegetables every 20 minutes for thorough and even cooking.

In a saucepan, heat stock with tomatoes until just simmering. Season liberally with salt and pepper.

Once vegetables are out of the oven, blend the vegetables, the warm stock and tomatoes, and sprigs of parsley in batches in a food processor or blender.

Next, in batches, strain soup through a very fine sieve or chinois. Push the soup through with a ladle, making sure to get all the liquid through.

Finally, in a large pot, bring all the strained soup up to a simmer. Taste and adjust seasoning.

This soup really benefits from a garnish for texture and contrast. I have used many different things for this soup, but I really love something sweet to balance the spice. Try diced red onion or corn sautéed in butter. I also like roasted cherry tomatoes cut in half and cilantro leaves.

Fresh Pappardelle with Roasted Eggplant, Ricotta Salata & Pine Nuts

Chef Roland A. Iadanza *(West Babylon, NY)*

Serves 4

> We like to include a pasta dish in addition to the expected egg dishes at brunch, enhanced with garden fresh vegetables and herbs. It is also an inexpensive way to stretch a dish to serve more people and be prepared ahead of time. It can be served hot or cold.

2 pounds fresh pappardelle

3 small Italian eggplants

⅓ cup extra virgin olive oil

1 tablespoon balsamic vinegar

1 clove garlic, crushed and minced

1 (14 ounce) can of artichoke hearts, cut in quarters

8 thin slices prosciutto

½ cup julienne sun-dried tomato

¼ cup fresh basil

2 cups baby arugula or spinach

¼ cup Kalamata olives, pitted

¼ cup toasted pine nuts

4 ounces shaved ricotta salata

Cut the eggplant into half-pieces, and place in a colander and salt. Drain over the bowl and toss twice. Remove and dry in a paper towel. Toss with olive oil, roast for 30 to 45 minutes, and stir often to cook evenly. Let it cool slightly. Whisk together olive oil, garlic, and balsamic vinegar. Place a large pot of water on the stove and bring to a boil. Salt the water and add fresh pasta. Cook al dente.

Place artichoke hearts, roasted eggplant, prosciutto, sun-dried tomatoes, and olives in large pasta bowl.

Add balsamic vinaigrette and pasta to artichoke mixture and toss, seasoning to taste with salt and pepper. Place shaved ricotta salata and pine nuts on top and serve.

Homemade Pizza

Monica

> This was a big hit with the adults at Cub Scout meetings. The boys preferred to add their own toppings, like sauce, mozzarella and pepperoni.

1 package ready-made pizza dough from your local pizzeria
Flour to dust surface
3 tablespoons extra virgin olive oil
½ cup pesto
½ cup sun-dried tomatoes, chopped fine
3 plum tomatoes, sliced thin
½ cup freshly grated parmesan cheese
½ cup mozzarella cheese
½ cup goat cheese
½ cup fresh oregano, finely chopped
Salt, pepper, and garlic powder to taste

Pesto
2 cups fresh basil
1 clove of garlic, pressed
½ cup pignoli nuts, chopped
½ cup parmesan cheese
¾ cup blended oil (see Chef's Tips) or olive oil

Cut pizza dough in quarters and roll out to 4 individual pizza crusts on a floured surface.

Brush with olive oil.

Place plum tomatoes over the entire surface.

Add a teaspoon alternately of the pesto, sun-dried tomatoes, and goat cheese on each pie.

Sprinkle with oregano, salt, pepper, garlic powder, and parmesan cheese, and finish with mozzarella.

Preheat your oven to 425°F and bake for 15 to 20 minutes or until the edges are golden brown.

Pesto

Mix together in a blender, and then use on the pizza as indicated above.

Refrigerate the unused portion and use for crudités or pasta dishes.

Part III

ENTRÉES & SIDES

ENTRÉES & SIDES

Having dinner together as a family is one of our most important social interactions. For many, gathering around the dinner table is a nurturing time together in an identifiable comfort zone. Dinner is a special opportunity for parents and children to connect and reflect on the day's events.

As mothers, we believe good habits begin at home. What happens at the table can set the tone for dinners to come. It is a microcosm of the meals you will one day share at school, as guests, or as adults in the workplace. Teaching our children table manners has been very important to us. Time at the dinner table is the opportunity to learn manners, how to converse, and how to share our meal.

Establishing a dinner time routine also helps to structure our days. Knowing that we will have a secure place to go at the end of each day provides comfort. Especially for children, meal time routines can help them to feel safer and more confident in taking on the world; this confidence will guide them to make more intelligent choices when they are on their own.

These special family moments are worth preserving, just as we take the time to preserve precious family heirlooms or ripened fruits off the vine. Whatever meals your family chooses for dinner, keep it happy, keep it healthy, and keep it up!

Smokey, Cheesy Quesadillas with Sweet Corn Relish

Erin Nicosia *(Artisanal Cheese Market, Sayville, NY)*

Serves 2-4

Once a week, the entire length of our Main Street was closed off for our year-round farmers' market. Local vendors sold their freshly grown fruits, vegetables, eggs, artisan breads, pastas, oils, and locally caught seafood. The sweet scent of fresh corn cut right off the cob is quintessential fall. It really brings out the farm girl in me. This event fostered a sense of community, while communicating the importance of supporting small, local farms, dairies, and businesses.

Being a huge foodie, my other favorite hangout was the cheese shop in town, where the lovely people behind the counter offered me samples. Determined to bring these experiences back to my hometown's farmers' market in Sayville, I began selling artisanal cheeses made in small batches on local farms, which used traditional methods. The result: a healthier environment and an incredibly delicious product.

Quesadillas

6 flour tortillas
1 cup cheddar, shredded
4 ounces sweet-fire red pepper-herbed chevre at room temperature
(as an alternative, use plain chevre and add crushed red pepper flakes to desired hotness)
1½ tablepoons basil, chopped
2 tablespoons canola oil
1 teaspoon chipotle chili powder
Kosher salt and freshly ground pepper to taste

Relish

2 ears sweet corn, roasted or grilled, and removed from the ears (see Chef's Tips)

¼ small red onion, finely chopped

1 tablespoon fresh basil, chopped

1 tablespoon balsamic vinegar

½ tablespoon honey

1 tablespoon canola oil

Kosher salt and freshly ground pepper to taste

Relish

For the corn relish, combine all ingredients and let sit while you build the quesadillas.

Quesadillas

Preheat oven to 425°F.

Heat a non-stick skillet on the stove and lightly crisp each tortilla on each side. Lay 4 of them out on a baking sheet.

Divide each of these: the goat cheese (it should be spreadable), the shredded cheddar, and the basil.

Sprinkle with salt, pepper, and chipotle chili powder.

Stack them to make 2 two-layer quesadillas, and top with the 2 remaining tortillas.

Sprinkle with some more cheddar and chili powder.

Bake for 8 to 10 minutes until the cheese is melted.

Top with corn relish, and enjoy.

Variation: Add veggies like mushrooms and zucchini, or any kind of meat you like.

Pan-Seared Duck Tacos with Habañero Mole and Tomatillo Salsa

Chef Phil Andriano *(New York, NY)*

Serves 1

> Food trends change as often as the weather. The current trend, locally resourced food items, is one that we hope will stick around. In the fall, the Tri-State area offers an abundance of local vegetables and herbs that increase the flavor of our recipes, because they are so fresh: from farm to table.

4 ounces duck breast, boneless and skinless
2 taco shells
¼ cup red onion, chopped
½ teaspoon habañero peppers, minced
2 tablespoons tomatillo, chopped
2 tablespoons plum tomato, chopped
1 teaspoon fresh cilantro, minced

½ ounce lime juice
½ teaspoon sugar
1 teaspoon semisweet chocolate
¼ cup chicken stock
1 tablespoon corn starch slurry (see Chef's Tips)
½ teaspoon cumin powder
½ teaspoon chili powder
2 teaspoons olive oil

In a skillet pan, sear the duck breast in 1 teaspoon of oil on all sides. Add half the onions and half the habanera peppers to the pan.

Sauté until the duck breast is finished, remove, and reserve just the duck breast. Add the lime juice and stock to the skillet with the onions and peppers. Add the cumin and chili powders along with the sugar and chocolate to thicken with the slurry.

To make salsa, combine the tomatillo, tomato, cilantro, remaining onions, and peppers with 1 teaspoon of oil. Mix well. Slice the duck breast into strips and toss in the mole sauce. Divide among the two taco shells and top with salsa.

Beef Stew

Amy Pawliw *(Plainview, NY)*

<u>Serves 6-8</u>

> Where I grew up in Forest Hills, Long Island, Halloween was always freezing cold. Exhausted after begging for treats, I always looked forward to going home and enjoying a steaming bowl of my mother's homemade beef stew, Italian bread, and orange Jell-O for dessert, in honor of the season. This became the traditional holiday meal, year after year. Now, as I prepare this meal for my family, it reminds me of the autumn nights when I was a child, coming home to my mother's warm kitchen.

Halloween Party Ideas

You can round out the festivities with holiday-themed drinks and main dishes for your guests. Try giving regular dishes funny names like "ghoulash," "Bloody Mary tomatoes," "chicken fingers," and "witches' brew." It is best to have designated adults taking turns as bartender when it is a party for both adults and children. That will free you up to enjoy the evening. Transform your coat closet into a costume closet, using hats, make-up, capes, wigs, and wings from Halloween's past, for guests who have arrived without a costume.

1-inch cubes beef stew meat
1 onion, chopped
1-2 cloves garlic, minced
3-4 cups water
2-3 beef bouillon, cubes
8 carrots, sliced
6 stalks of celery, diced
4 cups plum tomatoes, skinned and diced (or a 28-ounce can crushed tomatoes)
¾ cup red wine
3-4 potatoes, cubed
1½ cups fresh peas
Salt and pepper to taste

Brown beef in olive oil.

Add onion and garlic and brown well.

Add water, bouillon, chopped carrots, celery, the can of tomatoes, wine, salt, and pepper.

Add potatoes, and simmer for 1 hour.

Add peas, more salt, pepper, and wine to taste.

If needed to thicken, add a corn starch slurry (see Chef's Tips).

Mary's Beef "Ghoulash"

Mary Carlin *(East Meadow, NY)*

Serves 4-6

(Pairs well with Dumplings)

2 tablespoons butter or margarine

2 tablespoons salad oil

2 pounds boneless veal, or beef round or shoulder, cut into 1-inch cubes

1 cup sliced onion

1 cup green pepper strips

⅓ cup thinly sliced celery

1 clove garlic, crushed

1 cup thinly sliced carrots

2-3 teaspoons paprika

1½ teaspoons salt

⅛ teaspoon pepper

1 bay leaf

1 can condensed tomato soup or 1 (10½ ounce) can beef bouillon, undiluted

2 tablespoons tomato paste

2 tablespoons flour

½ cup sour cream

Heat 1 tablespoon butter and 1 tablespoon salad oil in a Dutch oven over medium heat. Add a few pieces of meat and brown on all sides. Remove to a bowl. Repeat with the rest of the meat, adding more oil and butter as needed.

In drippings, sauté (fry) green pepper, celery, and garlic until tender (about 3 minutes). Stir in carrots, paprika, salt, pepper, bay leaf, tomato soup (or bouillon), tomato paste, and browned meat.

Bring to a boil, and reduce heat. Simmer covered for 50 minutes or until the meat is fork-tender.

Remove the Dutch oven from the heat. With a slotted spoon, remove meat and vegetables to hot serving platter.

Pour pan liquid into a 1-cup measure; if necessary, add water to make 1 cup.

Add flour to the Dutch oven, and then gradually add reserved liquid, stirring constantly. Cook over moderate heat, stirring until mixture boils. Reduce heat, and simmer for 3 minutes.

Stir in sour cream. Heat slightly. Pour over meat and vegetables.

Serve with noodles, rice, or dumplings.

A Halloween Tradition

Kathleen Gallagher *(North Great River, NY)*

Each year, during October, I sit in a field to read stories to local children. The field is full of pumpkins and flowers at Papa's farm. The children come to pick their pumpkins and to sit with me to hear stories. Some children bring pictures of themselves sitting with me from years before. Some who had come to my story-telling years before now bring their own children to sit with me and have stories read to them. I enjoy watching how the children have grown from year to year and listening to their stories of how their lives are progressing. The pictures that they bring are a joy, although it is not as much fun to see how much I have aged over the years. It always amazes me that, one year, I am holding a baby who is staring up at me in my colorful costume, and then, in the blink of an eye, that very same child is fourteen-years-old and still sitting on my lap for their annual picture.

Parents and even grandparents also come to sit, dip their hand into my huge candy basket, and share some of their own stories. Before I go home and put my feet up, I pick a basket of tender green peppers and carrots from Papa's farm to use for that evening's dinner, and I reflect on the day as I eat my freshly picked meal.

Dumplings

Jim Bucko *(The Riverhouse at Goodspeed Station, Haddam, CT)*

> This recipe was a family favorite from my grandmother, Ann Bucko. It is a great dish from the "melting pot" section of Indiana. It is not nearly as much work as it sounds, but it does take time to prepare. Grandma used to cook tons of these dumplings to satisfy our appetites.

3 cups flour
1 tablespoon salt
3 eggs
1 cup water
3 quarts boiling water
4 tablespoons melted butter

Combine flour and salt in a large mixing bowl. Mix well with a wooden spoon. Add eggs and 1 cup of water. Beat with wooden spoon for 2 minutes or until there are no more lumps of egg and flour. Scrape the sides of the bowl. Dip cutting board into a boiling pot of water, remove board, and place ⅓ of dough on it.

Dip knife into boiling water, and then cut a narrow strip of dough about ¼-inch wide. Hold cutting board over the top of the pot and cut quickly with cutting and scraping motion. scraping the dough off the board into the boiling water.

When dumplings float to the top (allow to boil briefly for about 5 to 7 minutes), stir and remove the dumplings with a strainer. Place in casserole. Dribble melted butter over dumplings. Repeat until all dough is used. Mix thoroughly, so, all dumplings are coated with butter.

Oktoberfest festivals can be found and enjoyed all over the United States in the days leading up to October 1. Anyone who has ever attended one of these events will likely recall beer tents, picnic-style seating, omp-pa-pa bands, and, of course, traditional German food. It is a marvel how food prepared outdoors can taste so good.

Perfect Pork Roast

Mary Elizabeth

On Sundays, my husband Dennis and I often sit together, sipping coffee, listening to our favorite radio show, and looking through the paper to find the sales. Whenever we decided to make pork roast for dinner, our kids always asked, "Are you making Grandpa's sauerkraut?" My dad was very proud of his German heritage, and loved to cook traditional meals for us every October. One of our favorite Sunday meals growing up was roast pork and sauerkraut, using fresh marinated cabbage and apples. Thankfully, he wrote it down, so I am able to make it for my family today. It does not take long to make, and once you do, you will never go back to the canned alternative. Recently, my husband called our daughter, Nicole, to ask how she made the pork roast at the restaurant where she works. I laughed to myself, thinking back to when we first married and I would call my parents for their guidance on how to make a particular meal. Now, we have come full circle.

(Pairs well with Sauerkraut)

Pork (boneless tenderloin)

Blended oil (see Chef's Tips)

Salt and freshly cracked pepper to taste

Preheat the oven to 400°F.

Rub blended oil over the pork (boneless tenderloin).

Generously season with salt and freshly cracked pepper.

Heat large skillet/roasting pan/griddle over two burners on stove-top.

Place the pork on the griddle and sear (you should hear a sizzle; if not, then the pan is not hot enough, so, remove the pork and wait until it is ready).

Sear each side (approximately 3 minutes for each side) until golden brown and crisp, rolling the loin until the entire surface is golden brown. Remove from the pan.

Place the loin on a roasting rack in a roasting pan.

Bake in the oven for approximately 20 minutes per pound, until the thermometer reads 150°F.

Note

If the crust begins to darken before the internal temperature reads 150°F, loosely cover the surface of the loin with aluminum foil.

Grandpa's Sauerkraut

Christian Raiser *(Lynbrook, NY)*

<u>Serves 8</u>

1 (16 ounce) bag sauerkraut, rinsed well
1 medium green apple, chopped
1 small onion, chopped
1 small carrot, chopped
2 tablespoons butter
½ cup chicken broth
½ cup white wine (chardonnay)
½ teaspoon white vinegar

Sauté onion, apple, and carrot in butter for 10 minutes.

Add remaining ingredients and simmer on low heat.

Add sugar to taste.

Leftovers may be stored in the refrigerator in a canning jar for 2 weeks.

Mom's Sauerbraten

Olive Kopp *(Hicksville, NY)*

<u>Serves 6</u>

(Pairs well with Red Cabbage & Dumplings)

4 pounds bottom round (can also use cross rib, shoulder, or top round)
1 cup vinegar
1 cup water
1 tablespoon allspice
1 teaspoon whole cloves
½ teaspoon thyme
1 bay leaf
4 ginger snaps, crushed
1 medium onion, sliced or chopped
¼ cup raisins
2 tablespoons corn starch
Salt and pepper to taste

Marinade

Add all ingredients, except for the corn starch, to a bowl large enough to fit the meat. Note: marinade should cover three-quarters of the meat.

Cover the bowl tightly with plastic wrap and place in the refrigerator for 3 to 4 days before cooking.

Turn every day.

Strain marinade, reserving some onions and raisins. Save to make the gravy.

Oil bottom of the pot, and brown all sides of the meat well.

Add ¾ cup of water, cover, and simmer for approximately 2 hours.

Remove the meat from the pot when done.

Gravy

Pour strained marinade back into the pot with the reserved onions and raisins.

Add an additional ¾ cup of water.

In a separate bowl, make slurry by mixing with a spoon 2 tablespoons of corn starch and ⅓ cup of cold water.

Pour the slurry into the pot and bring to a boil. Your gravy will slowly become thick as you stir it.

You can add a few crushed ginger snaps and raisins if desired to the gravy.

Red Cabbage with Apples

2½ pounds head red cabbage, shredded
¾ cup boiling water
3 large apples, sliced
3 tablespoons melted butter
1½ teaspoons flour
⅓ cup vinegar
¼ cup brown sugar
¼ teaspoon salt
¼ teaspoon pepper

Put cabbage in a large pot, add boiling water, and cover for 15 minutes.

Add the rest of the ingredients, combine, and heat over a low flame for approximately 45 minutes.

An Idea for Meal Time

To get conversation going at the dinner table, ask your children what their favorite part of the day was. For Monica's son, she remembers his was usually lunch or gym. Then ask them why. Was it the leisurely fun aspect, or maybe because they got to see friends who were not in their regular classes? Ask them what they did for fun, what they learned, or what they would like to do next. Dinner-time is also a perfect opportunity to talk about relatives or friends who your children may not see that often, helping them to remember good times and keep the person close to them in their hearts.

Herbed Angel Hair with Wilted Radicchio

Chef Heather Merriken *(Camden, ME)*

During the fall season, bitter greens such as radicchio, endive, and escarole make an appearance in salads and as a welcome accompaniment to braised and roasted meats. After heavy meals, I find that adding antioxidant-packed greens and bright, fresh citrus to my favorite comfort foods lets me feel a bit lighter and more energized. For an added boost, use whole grain or Omega-3 pasta in place of regular angel hair.

6 tablespoons butter
3 tablespoons garlic-infused olive oil
1 yellow onion, sliced thinly
2 heads Treviso radicchio or other
Bitter greens, cut into ¼-inch wide strips
(discarding fully white parts)
5 sprigs rosemary
7 leaves fresh sage
2 tablespoons fresh parsley
2 tablespoons fresh chervil
2 tablespoons fresh tarragon
1 tablespoon fresh thyme
2 lemons
1 blood orange
1½ pounds angel hair pasta
Kosher salt and freshly ground pepper to taste

Place a 6-quart pot of cool, fresh water on the stove on high heat. Add ¼ cup of salt. Cover and bring to a rolling boil.

In the meantime, pick and coarsely chop all the herbs, keeping rosemary and sage. Separate. Zest lemons and blood orange. Juice 1½ lemons and the blood orange. Reserve.

Cut butter into small pieces. Add butter and olive oil to large sauté pan over medium-low heat. Once butter is melted, add onion and toss. Season liberally with salt and pepper.

After onions become translucent (approximately 5 to 7 minutes), add chopped rosemary and sage. Toss to coat onions evenly with herbs.

Add angel hair to boiling water. Stir rapidly with tongs for 1 minute to prevent pasta from sticking together. Bring pasta to al dente firmness (about 7 minutes).

Add Treviso radicchio to the pan and toss. Cook for 1 minute on medium heat. Then add angel hair and 1 cup of pasta water to sauté pan. Stir. Cook for 1 minute to let the pasta absorb the flavors in the pan.

Finally add zests, citrus juice, and remaining herbs. Adjust seasoning with salt and pepper. Toss and serve immediately.

Baked Penne Pasta with Caramelized Onions, Mushrooms, and Spinach

J'ne Autry Dove *(Canyon, CA)*

1 pound penne pasta
1 tablespoon olive oil
3 tablespoons butter
2 large white onions, sliced
½ pound bacon
1 pound cremini mushrooms, trim stems and coarsely chop
1 tablespoon garlic, chopped
2 cups whipping cream (for a healthy alternative, use ½ chicken stock and ½ cream)
10 ounces fresh baby spinach
1 tablespoon fresh thyme, stems removed and chopped
1 cup parmesan-reggiano cheese, freshly grated
Salt and pepper to taste

Preheat oven to 400°F. Grease a large 3-quart baking dish.

Cook pasta in boiling water for 6 minutes (slightly under-done, since it will be baking later), drain, and toss with olive oil. Keep in a large bowl.

Melt butter in a large skillet and sauté onions very slowly until caramelized (about 1 hour or so). Transfer the onions to a small bowl and set aside (you can do this step in advance).

In the same skillet, fry bacon until crisp, transfer bacon to a plate with a paper towel, and leave bacon fat in pan.

Sauté mushrooms in bacon fat for 10 minutes, add garlic, cook for another minute, add onions back to skillet, and add cream. Simmer for 10 minutes on low heat until thickened. Stir in ½ cup of parmesan cheese and pour entire mixture over pasta along with the spinach and fresh thyme.

Pour into a prepared baking dish, and sprinkle remaining parmesan cheese over top. Cover tightly with foil and bake for 10 to 15 minutes. Take the foil off, and bake for 8 to 10 minutes longer until bubbly hot.

Penne and Roasted Butternut Squash with Sage and Chevre

Erin Nicosia *(Sayville, NY)*

<u>Serves 4-6</u>

1 medium butternut squash, peeled and cubed into bite-size pieces
1 small bunch fresh sage, chopped
2 cloves garlic, minced
4½ ounces chevre, crumbled and at room temperature
1 pound pasta
Extra virgin olive oil to taste
Salt and freshly ground pepper to taste
Freshly grated nutmeg to taste

In a bowl, toss the butternut squash with some extra virgin olive oil, salt, pepper, sage, garlic, and nutmeg.

Begin boiling some water for the pasta.

Roast the squash in a 400°F oven, tossing once or twice until golden brown and the edges start to crisp (about 30 to 40 minutes).

Cook the penne (or pasta of your choice; orecchiette is great for this too) in salted water until al dente and drain.

Toss the hot pasta with the squash mixture and top with chevre. Serve immediately.

Roasted Red Pepper Lasagna

Chef Heather Merriken *(Camden, ME)*

> Growing up in a predominately Italian-American community, meatballs and spaghetti were a staple for Sunday night dinners. Likewise, special occasions were never without lasagna. My brother found out a few years ago that he is allergic to tomatoes, so I developed this recipe for him. He gets his own private pan made with fresh red peppers harvested locally and bought at a nearby farm stand.

6 cups roasted red peppers, jarred or freshly roasted, peeled and seeded
1 quart heavy cream
2 cups whole milk
Parmigiana-reggiano cheese, grated
1 (1 pound) ball of good quality mozzarella, sliced thinly and seasoned generously with salt and pepper
1 quart whole milk ricotta cheese
1 bunch fresh basil leaves, washed and torn or chopped
1 (1 pound) box lasagna
Good quality olive oil
Dried oregano
1 head of garlic, roasted
Red chili flakes
Fresh or frozen spinach (optional)
Kosher salt and freshly ground pepper to taste

Preheat oven to 350°F. Roast garlic according to directions on the left. In the meantime, in a large bowl, combine ricotta, 2 tablespoons of salt, 1 tablespoon of pepper, 1 tablespoon of oregano, ¼ cup of basil, and ¼ cup of olive oil. Stir until well combined. Set aside.

In a medium-sized pot, add the cream, milk, and 10 cloves of roasted garlic. To get the garlic out of its skin, simply pinch at the base and squeeze or scoop it out with a butter knife.

Bring the cream mixture to a boil, stirring the liquid about once a minute. As you stir, make sure to scrape the bottom and sides of the pot with a rubber spatula, so the cream does not stick and burn.

Once cream mixture comes to a boil, turn heat down to low. Stir in 2 tablespoons of salt, 1 teaspoon of pepper, 1 teaspoon of red chili flakes, and 1 teaspoon of oregano. Simmer for about 10 minutes, stirring occasionally.

The cream mixture will have thickened at this point. Taste and adjust seasoning.

Pour the cream mixture into a blender with sliced roasted red peppers and ½ cup of parmigiano-reggiano cheese. If using jarred peppers, strain excess water off, first. Blend ingredients until thoroughly combined, making sure to scrape down the sides of the blender with a rubber spatula to incorporate any chunks. The final mixture should be creamy and smooth.

Drizzle a little olive oil on the bottom of the lasagna pan. Put one single layer of lasagna noodles down close together, but not overlapping. If you need to break the noodles in half to cover the entire bottom of pan, do so.

Pour some of the red pepper sauce on top of the lasagna noodles, coating generously (approximately ¾ cup). Scoop tablespoons of the herbed ricotta on top of this, dotting evenly. No need to spread it around. If using spinach, distribute a thin, but even layer.

Add another single layer of lasagna noodles, but this time, in the opposite direction, creating a thatched effect.

Pour a little more sauce on. Add a single layer of the seasoned mozzarella cheese and a sprinkling of parmigiana-reggiano cheese.

Continue layering until the pan is full: about half from the top lip, alternating the direction of the noodles and ingredients.

Top lasagna with remaining sauce. Cover loosely with aluminum foil and place in a heated oven for 40 minutes.

Turn oven up to 425°F. Remove the foil from the pan and add some mozzarella cheese and a sprinkling of parmigiana-reggiano cheese to the top of the lasagna. Cook for 10 more minutes or until the cheese is melted and lightly browned. Garnish with the rest of the torn basil leaves and serve with toasty bread.

Using a thatched pattern will help the lasagna hold together when you slice up a piece and try to get it out of the pan. Push dry noodles down to release any trapped air and to help the ricotta distribute itself.

Roasting Red Peppers

If you have a gas stove-top, turn the stove on high and place peppers directly on the flame, allowing the skin to char black before rotating. If you do not have a gas stove-top, you can grill them for approximately 3 to 5 minutes on each side until the entire pepper has charred. Immediately place in a brown paper bag and close tightly, or place in a metal mixing bowl and cover tightly with plastic wrap. Leave hot peppers covered for at least 20 minutes to allow the heat from the peppers to create steam and loosen the skin. Then, using your hands or a paper towel, simply peel or wipe off the charred skin. Do not rinse under water, or you will wash off the roasted flavor.

You can also put your oven on 450°F (broiler setting), wipe the peppers with vegetable oil, and sprinkle with salt and pepper, coating evenly. Place on a sheet tray on the top rack directly under the broiler. Rotate the peppers every 5 minutes until their entire surface is black. Then follow the same directions as above.

Linguini with Little Neck Clams & Vegetables

Chef Joseph DeNicola *(La Tavola Restaurant, Sayville, NY)*

I remember one time that my brother had brought home a half-dozen fish and four dozen clams that he had caught, leaving it to me to prepare them. I was sixteen-years-old. Having spent many hours standing at my mom's side as she cooked, I knew how to make a sauce and bake the fish. My mother fled the kitchen, terrified, as we all laughed and I bravely gutted the fish. It is similar to preparing a chicken for chicken cutlets—discard all of the insides, get rid of the bones, and clean before cooking. *(Story by Monica)*

24 Little Neck clams
1 pound linguini
2 medium zucchini, cut into half-moons
2 medium yellow squash, cut into half-moons
8 ounces pancetta
2 tablespoons garlic
4 ounces fresh basil, sliced
15 red and yellow cherry tomatoes, halved
1 cup lemon juice
2 cups white wine
4 ounces extra virgin olive oil
½ cup clam broth

Sauté pancetta in olive oil until crispy. Add garlic and vegetables and sauté until golden brown. Add lemon juice, white wine, and clam broth.

Bring to a boil. Add clams. Let them steam until they open.

Add fresh basil.

In a separate pot, boil linguini in salted water. Strain the pasta and place in a serving bowl.

Arrange clams, vegetables, and sauce on top of pasta.

Seared Maine Diver Sea Scallops over Butternut Squash Risotto with Pancetta & Fresh Sage

Chef Joseph DeNicola *(La Tavola Restaurant, Sayville, NY)*

Saffron Broth

1 onion, chopped

2 celery stalks, chopped

1 carrot, chopped

1 bay leaf

5 black peppercorns

1 quart chicken stock

4 roasted garlic cloves, crushed

½ cup Pernot

½ tablespoon saffron

Risotto

2 cups risotto (arborio rice)

4 fresh sage leaves, thinly sliced

1 onion, chopped

½ cup diced pancetta

1 cup heavy cream

½ cup parmesan cheese

4 ounces butter

1 quart chicken stock

Roasted Butternut Squash

1 butternut squash

3 tablespoons olive oil

Salt and pepper to taste

Scallops

16 U-10 diver sea scallops, dry

2 tablespoons olive oil

Saffron Broth

In chicken stock, boil onion, celery, and carrot with bay leaf and peppercorns for 30 minutes. Strain, return to the pot, and add saffron, Pernot, and garlic cloves. Reduce for 5 minutes and let it cool. Season with salt and white pepper.

Risotto

Cook pancetta until crispy. Then add onion and sauté until soft. Add rice, and coat with oil and pancetta. Slowly add the stock and stir constantly for 16 to 20 minutes. Finish with cheese, cream, sage, and butter. Season with salt and pepper. Risotto should be al dente, but not hard.

Roasted Butternut Squash

Peel and seed butternut squash. Cut into 1-inch cubes in a bowl. Mix with olive oil, salt, and pepper. Roast on a baking sheet for 20 minutes at 350°F.

Scallops

Heat skillet or heavy-duty frying pan until ripping hot. Heat oil. Sear scallops on both sides until brown and cooked through.

Add roasted squash to risotto. Place in the center of the bowl. Arrange scallops on the risotto. Add saffron broth. Garnish with whole sage leaves.

Baked Salmon and Creamed Spinach Provençal

Polly Talbott *(Lynbrook, NY)*

<u>Serves 6</u>

2 pounds spinach, washed and stemmed

2 tablespoons butter

2 tablespoons flour

2 cups milk

¾ teaspoon salt

⅛ teaspoon pepper

¼ teaspoon freshly grated nutmeg

⅛ teaspoon ground cloves

2 pounds salmon fillet, cut into 6 servings, rinsed and patted dry

3 tablespoons extra virgin olive oil

1 small clove garlic, minced

¼ teaspoon salt

2 ripe tomatoes, peeled, seeded, and diced

Preheat oven to 400°F. Place spinach in a large saucepan over medium heat and cook covered in the water clinging to the leaves until wilted (4 to 5 minutes). Remove to a colander, rinse quickly, and press out as much water as possible. Finely chop, and set aside.

In a 2-quart saucepan, heat the butter and whisk in the flour until smooth. Whisk in the milk. Cook over medium heat, stirring frequently until the mixture comes to a boil. Remove from the heat. Stir in ½ teaspoon of the salt, pepper, nutmeg, and cloves; stir in the spinach.

Brush salmon with 1 tablespoon of olive oil and season with the remaining ¼ teaspoon of salt and ⅛ teaspoon of pepper.

Divide creamed spinach among the 6 buttered gratin dishes. Nestle a salmon fillet in each. Bake for 18 minutes or until the salmon flakes easily on the top, but is still slightly mushy on the inside. If you like, you can broil the salmon to brown it off.

Mash minced garlic and ¼ teaspoon of salt on a cutting board to puree garlic. Combine mashed garlic, tomato, and the remaining 2 tablespoons of olive oil; stir to combine. Garnish each serving of salmon with chopped tomato after it is baked.

To bake in a large ceramic baking dish, spread the spinach mixture on the bottom of the dish, portion the salmon, and place on top of the spinach; bake as stated in the recipe. Serve with spinach still on the bottom, and spoon tomatoes on top.

Seafood and Zucchini Medley á la Italy

Ben Colvin *(Remsenburg, NY)*

(Pairs well with Roasted Potatoes)

> While traveling on business and for pleasure in Italy, I learned that part of the art of their cuisine is that less is more when local, in-season ingredients are used. This was true whether I was in the Tuscan countryside or in the city of Rome.

1 tablespoon butter
1 pound peeled shrimp or scallops
1 tablespoon olive oil
1 shallot
2 cloves garlic
Fresh thyme to taste
2 medium-sized zucchini: 1 green, 1 yellow (for color), shred to spaghetti-like consistency

Preheat a Teflon pan over low heat. Then add butter, and add olive oil when the butter stops foaming.

Add shallot, sauté for 2 to 3 minutes, and then add garlic until fragrant – do not let it brown.

Add shrimp or scallops and sauté until browned and cooked through. Add pepper to taste and remove from the skillet.

In the skillet, add the shredded zucchini, thyme, and pepper (do not salt until cooked).

Sauté until browned. Add salt to taste.

Serve with shrimp or scallops on top.

Healthy Alternative

Try using shredded zucchini instead of pasta, or try spaghetti squash. It is very easy to prepare (the produce department typically slaps a "how-to" label on the skin). You will not believe your eyes when you start to pull out the spaghetti-like strands from the squash with your fork. It does not exactly taste like pasta, but the consistency is very similar, and, with a generous amount of your favorite sauce, you won't notice a difference.

Roasted Potatoes

Ben Colvin *(Remsenburg, NY)*

> With my simple Seafood and Zucchini Medley, I often serve roasted potatoes. I like to use a mix of smaller Red Bliss and Yukon gold to add color to the plate.

Small Red Bliss and Yukon gold potatoes
Butter and olive oil
2-3 cloves garlic, crushed
Fresh rosemary sprigs to taste
Salt and freshly cracked pepper to taste

In a roasting pan, add butter and olive oil, heat in the oven until melted, mix in the potatoes, and coat.

Add salt, pepper, garlic, and some rosemary to taste.

When done (fork will easily pierce through the potatoes), remove the garlic and rosemary.

Serve with some fresh rosemary on top for a garnish.

Gnocchi with Brown Butter Sauce

Darcy Paige *(Mystic, CT)*

This recipe is from my nana, whose parents settled in Mystic from Fomo di Zoldo, Italy. She would make gnocchi for family gatherings during the fall and winter months. The long preparation was part of the fun, as it got the family working together, providing lots of time to chat. The kids loved it, as it was like rolling and cutting chunks of Play-Doh. We would have it with Nana's favorite browned butter or homemade marinara sauce and a salad.

1 pound Russet potatoes, peeled
1½ cups flour
1 egg
¼ teaspoon salt

Boil potatoes until soft, and mix with all the ingredients.

Roll on a floured surface ("long snake"), and cut into small wedges.

Keep uncooked, cut floured dough, and spread out until ready to cook.

Boil large kettle of water with approximately 1 teaspoon of salt.

Add a portion of the gnocchi, and cook until they float to the top (approximately 10 minutes).

Scoop out cooked gnocchi, and repeat with remaining uncooked gnocchi.

Serve with Browned Butter

Melt 1 stick of sweet butter in a pan until it actually starts to brown. Immediately take off the heat, and pour over the gnocchi before serving.

Roasted Curried Squash

Carolyn Schaeffer *(Doylestown, PA)*

> This dish goes great with a pan-seared fish like halibut or tilapia, or can be served over rice or quinoa for a hearty vegetarian meal.

1 butternut squash
1 large carrot
1 medium onion
1-3 cloves garlic
1-2 tablespoons oil
2 tablespoons yellow curry powder
1 teaspoon garam masala
Kosher salt and pepper to taste

Preheat the oven to 400°F.

Peel and cube the squash and carrot, and chop the onion into chunks.

Chop the garlic and toss with the vegetables in an 8 x 11½-inch glass baking dish.

Drizzle with oil, and sprinkle on the curry powder, garam masala, salt, and pepper. Toss well with a wooden spoon or two.

Cover loosely with aluminum foil and roast for 15 minutes. Stir, remove the foil, and roast for 10 to 15 minutes uncovered until the vegetables reach your desired tenderness.

Drizzle with maple syrup when done if you like your squash super sweet and delicious.

If you do not have garam masala in your pantry, and do not have the time to stop at your local market, you can easily make it. Here is a simple recipe:

Mix the following ingredients and store in a spice jar:
½ teaspoon cumin, ½ teaspoon paprika, ¼ teaspoon cinnamon, ¼ teaspoon cayenne pepper, ¼ teaspoon crumbled bay leaves, ⅛ teaspoon ground cloves

Garden Herbed Seared Chicken with Red Pepper Sauce

Chef Nicole Roarke *(Blue Point, NY)*

8 pounds boneless and skinless chicken breasts
1½ cups olive oil
1½ quarts heavy cream
1 quart chicken stock (see Chef's Tips)
2 pounds fresh red peppers, roasted (see Chef Tips) or 2 (16 ounce) jars roasted red peppers, drained and pureed
½ cup roasted red peppers (for garnish)
4 tablespoons butter
4 tablespoons flour
1 tablespoon freshly chopped or 1 teaspoon dried thyme
1 cup garlic cloves, roasted (see Chef Tips)
Garlic oil (reserved from roasting)
3 shallots, minced
¾ cup sherry or white wine
1 teaspoon dried Italian seasoning
1 teaspoon garlic and onion powder
2 tablespoons sugar
Parmesan cheese (optional)
Salt, freshly cracked pepper, and crushed red pepper flakes to taste

Preheat oven to 350°F.

Using a blender or food processor, puree drained red peppers and roasted garlic.

Trim excess fat off the chicken, as needed.

Marinate chicken in reserved garlic oil, salt, pepper, dried Italian seasonings, and garlic and onion powder for ½ hour.

Heat grill pan (or non-stick skillet), and sear the chicken for 2 minutes on each side (do not overcook).

Lay the chicken pieces on a sheet pan, and pour 1 cup of chicken stock over it.

Bake the chicken for 15 to 20 minutes.

Remove the chicken and let it cool. Add 3 tablespoons of olive oil in a large pot, and place over medium heat.

Sauté shallots, salt, pepper, crushed red pepper, sugar, and thyme.

Add the pureed red pepper and roasted garlic mixture.

Add sherry and the remaining chicken stock, and bring to a boil.

In a separate pan, make a roux (see Chef Tips).

Add roux to the sauce and bring to a boil. Add cream and mix well.

Dice chicken and add to the sauce.

Sprinkle freshly grated parmesan cheese on top, if desired, before serving.

Serve over cooked pasta or rice.

A Time-Saving Tip

Cook up about a dozen thinly sliced cutlets at a time, breading, sautéing, and serving them the first night, then freezing them to be served another time.

Athenian Chicken with Fresh Herbs

Paula Gottlieb Herman *(Westbury, NY)*

(Pairs well with Taboulleh)

> This recipe means the world to me because it came from my mother Elaine Esther Gottlieb. My mom was an amazing cook from the old school who never measured any ingredients, yet her food was always consistently delicious. For this recipe, I sat her down in my kitchen, and as she assembled the ingredients, I measured her palm-full of salt and her pinches of oregano or paprika. I had her splash the olive oil into an empty bowl, so I could measure it with a tablespoon. This dish made it into a collection of recipes given to me by family and friends at my bridal shower. It is a warm and delicious entrée that is amazing when served over rice with a drizzle of garlicky oil.

1 fryer chicken, skinned and cut into eighths
5 cloves garlic, sliced
Juice of 1 lemon
3 tablespoons olive oil
2 teaspoons kosher salt
½ teaspoon paprika
¼ teaspoon dried oregano

Wash chicken, dry thoroughly. Into a mixing bowl, put the chicken, sliced garlic, salt, lemon, olive oil, paprika, and oregano.

Mix thoroughly. Make sure the chicken is coated completely. Place the covered bowl in the refrigerator overnight to marinate. Turn the chicken in the marinade a few times.

Line oven-safe pan with tin foil. Place the chicken in the pan. Spread the remaining garlic and spices on the chicken.

Preheat the oven to 350°F. Bake the chicken for 30 minutes or until the chicken has a good color and there is no pink or white fluid coming out. Retain and separate garlicky oil (gravy from baked chicken pan). Discard excess fat.

Serve over a bed of rice with collected garlicky oil.

Eggplant Boats

Chef Alex Davis *(Furci's Brick Oven Pizza, Bayport, NY)*

4 medium eggplants
1 medium onion, finely chopped
½ cup unseasoned bread crumbs
1 tablespoon butter
1 cup parmesan cheese, freshly grated
1-2 tablespoons fresh oregano, finely chopped

Preheat oven to 350°F.

Hollow out the middle and retain.

Hull the eggplant skin, leaving about ⅛-inch of the flesh to maintain its shape.

In an 18-inch skillet, brown the onion until translucent (about 10 minutes on low heat).

Add the chopped-up eggplant flesh, breadcrumbs, and butter.

Sauté until soft.

Put mixture back into the prepared eggplant shells.

Top with a generous amount of parmesan cheese and oregano.

Bake until the top is golden brown.

Pasta and Broccoli

Monica

After a long day hiking outdoors on a weekend or when short of time after work, pasta and broccoli is a satisfying and healthy quick dish to prepare. When we cannot think of what to have for dinner, it is always my son's first choice.

This is an Italian dish that I learned from my mother. My mom makes hers a little soupy by using some of the water her broccoli had been cooked in. I make mine drier because I never cook vegetables in water. Instead, I either steam or microwave them to retain more texture, color, and vitamins.

1 large head broccoli florets and stems
½ cup extra virgin olive oil
4-8 cloves fresh, crushed garlic (depending upon your palette)
1-1½ cups grated romano or parmesan cheese
1 package thin, whole wheat pasta (our favorite, but you can use spaghetti, linguini, or even rotelli if it is used as a side dish)

Wash and prepare your broccoli, trimming the florets and stems of their chewy outer skin, and cutting into bite-size pieces.

Steam or microwave for 10 to 15 minutes (depending on your desired texture).

Put in a large bowl and mix with a quarter of the olive oil, garlic, and cheese. Set aside.

Boil your pasta according to the package directions, drain, and mix in half of the remaining olive oil, garlic, and cheese (in that order).

Combine the broccoli and pasta in a large pasta bowl, adding in the remaining olive oil, garlic, and cheese. Mix thoroughly and serve.

More cheese can be added to suit individual tastes at the table.

For the soupy version, boil your broccoli in water and follow the same directions as above, using as much or as little of the broccoli water to suit your taste.

Italian Meatballs

Monica

When I was in elementary school, my mom worked in the kitchen at a local restaurant, which was owned by my friend's parents. It was very homey on a street with just five houses on it, tucked in among several factories in East New York, with just a few tables and a small counter—a combination between a neighborhood diner and truck stop at lunch-time (we all know that truckers know the best places to find home cooking, and this was just such a place).

Many an afternoon after school, we would pop in at the back door of the kitchen and sample Italian bread dipped in sauce or sautéed meatballs ready to be dropped into the pot for the spaghetti and meatballs on the menu the next day.

The head cook had been in the merchant marines, and ran an elaborate, efficient kitchen. My mother, already a great cook, took away several recipes that are still our family staples today.

1 pound lean, ground sirloin
1 large yellow onion
1 large egg
2-3 cloves minced garlic
⅛ cup fresh parsley, chopped fine, or 2 tablespoons dried parsley
⅛ cup fresh oregano (or 1 teaspoon oregano)
1 cup seasoned bread crumbs
½ cup parmesan or romano cheese
Extra virgin olive oil enough to sauté
Salt and pepper to taste

Mix all of your ingredients (except the olive oil), and roll into balls about 1 inch in diameter. Brown your meatballs in the olive oil; do not cook them all the way through.

Drain your sautéed meatballs on paper towels to get off the excess oil, and drop them carefully one at a time into your sauce (see the next recipe for the sauce). Cover and simmer for no less than 2 hours (ideally 3 hours).

Serve with your favorite pasta (although, when I first had these meatballs, it was called spaghetti) and a salad.

Sunday Dinner Spaghetti Sauce

Betty Meyers *(Port Jefferson, NY)*

This recipe is from my father's side of the family, taught to my mom by his sister when she was a young bride. This spaghetti sauce has to be made when you have the time to hover over it and stir it for no less than three hours, carefully skimming the top for any excess oil from the meatballs.

Our house was not the only one having this on a Sunday; almost every Italian family on our street had some version at varying times of day. We usually ate at about 5:00 or 6:00 p.m., because my mother was a working mom and needed the rest of her Sunday to oversee and complete the weekly chores. My next-door neighbor ate at her grandmother's with the whole extended family at 1:00 p.m. sharp. They called their sauce "gravy," and it had a mix of beef bones or sausage mixed in.
(Story by Monica)

Extra virgin olive oil
1 large onion, chopped
5-6 cloves garlic, sliced
1 (28 ounce) can tomato puree and 1 (28 ounce) can water
6-8 plum tomatoes, skinned and diced, and 1 (28 ounce) can water
1 (6 ounce) can tomato paste and 1 (6 ounce) can water
½ cup fresh oregano, chopped fine, or 2-3 tablespoons dried oregano

In a large sauce pot, cook your onion until translucent, and then the garlic.

Add the tomato puree, fresh tomatoes, tomato paste, and water.

Sprinkle the oregano over the top and stir.

Place your prepared meatballs in, bring to a boil, and then immediately reduce the heat and cover.

Simmer for 3 hours, stirring from the bottom of the pot to reduce sticking.

Skim the top of any excess oil rising to the surface.

Grandma Reger's Meatloaf

Monica

(Pairs well with Mushroom Gravy & Potato Pancakes)

My Irish-German grandmother cooked simple meals like pot roast, meatloaf, and codfish cakes on Fridays. I was six-years-old the last time that I tasted her food. I had just come in from collecting leaves and was chilled to the bone, only to find a comforting dish of meatloaf and creamy mashed potatoes as my payment for a job well-done.

In my twenties, I recreated her meatloaf in my own kitchen and surprised the family at dinner. My mom instantly recognized it and asked, "How did you come up with this?" "From memory," I answered. Today I either use lean ground sirloin, buffalo, or turkey. My mother and son like to have mushroom gravy with theirs. The gravy takes no more than five minutes to make. You can double, triple, or quadruple the ingredients to accommodate more people.

When making turkey meatloaf, use one cup each of shredded celery, carrot, and a pinch of thyme to the recipe. To make the turkey gravy, use chicken stock and omit the Gravy Master©.

1 pound ground sirloin or buffalo
1 medium yellow onion, quartered and sliced
1 egg
1 cup flavored bread crumbs

Mix all the ingredients in the order written above into a ball.

Shape into a loaf about 1 to 1½-inches high in an 8 x 11½ x 2-inch baking dish.

Bake at 350°F for approximately 1 hour.

Let it sit for a few minutes and serve immediately.

Mushroom Gravy

1 box white button mushrooms (about 16-20), sliced
1-2 tablespoons butter
1 cup homemade or commercial beef stock
¼ cup freshly chopped parsley
1-2 tablespoons flour
1 drop Gravy Master©

Sauté mushrooms in butter until they begin to soften.

Stir in the beef stock, let the flavors combine, and then add parsley.

Thicken the above with 1 to 2 tablespoons of flour mixed with a little of your cooking broth, making a thin paste.

Gently boil down, stirring constantly to your desired thickness.

Stir in a drop of Gravy Master©.

Gravy Master© is a concentrated liquid additive blend of spices and caramel color, used to brown sauces. It can be found in your local supermarket in the seasoning aisle.

German Potato Pancakes

Monica

Whenever my mom made potato pancakes, it was a miracle if they even made it to the table. We kids would hover around her in the kitchen, snatching them as quickly as she cooked them. Preparing them was a labor of love, as she hand-grated the potatoes, trying not to scrape her fingers.

2 pounds potatoes
2 eggs, beaten
1 medium to large yellow onion
¼ cup all-purpose flour (add flour to batter as needed)
1 teaspoon salt
¼ cup butter

Shred potatoes and drain off any excess liquid that has accumulated.

Mix your potatoes, eggs, onion, flour, and salt.

Heat 2 tablespoons of butter over medium heat.

Pour in about ¼ cup of batter for each pancake, maneuvering them into about 4-inch circles in the skillet.

Cook until golden brown (about 2 minutes on each side).

Drain on paper towels.

Keep warm in the oven as you use up the remaining batter, adding butter as needed.

Hearty Chicken Pot Pie

Irene Yee *(Aqueboque, NY)*

<u>Serves 6</u>

10 ounces chicken stock (see Chef's Tips) or 1 can condensed chicken broth
1¾ cup water (divided)
4 medium carrots, thinly sliced
3 medium red potatoes, diced
2 cups mushrooms, quartered
1 medium onion, coarsely chopped
1 cup fresh peas (or frozen)
⅓ cup flour
1 unbaked 9-inch pie crust (see Pâté Brisée recipe on page 18)
2 tablespoons olive oil
2½ cups cooked chicken, cooled and cut into 1-inch cubes

Preheat oven to 425°F.

Combine the broth, 1 cup of water, carrots, and potatoes in a medium saucepan. Bring to a boil, reduce the heat, and simmer over low heat for 10 minutes.

Heat the oil in a large skillet over medium heat. Add mushrooms and onions. Sauté until softened (about 5 minutes). Stir in the broth mixture and peas.

In a small preparation bowl, whisk the remaining ⅓ cup of water into the flour until smooth. Whisk into the vegetable mixture, increasing the heat to medium-high, and bringing to a boil until the mixture has thickened.

Roll out your dough large enough to be a 10-inch circle or to top your baking dish. Stir the cooked chicken into the vegetable mixture, and then transfer to the baking dish.

Place the pie crust on top, and rim and flute the edge. Cut a scalloped round from the center with a cookie cutter or sharp knife.

Bake until bubbly and the crust is brown (about 20 minutes). Serve with crusty bread.

Fall Stew

Mary Elizabeth

<u>Serves 6-8</u>

Each week, my dad would pick a recipe from the Wednesday *New York Times*, and then he and my mom would spend the next few days going on a scavenger hunt around town until they found all the ingredients. It was easy to find fresh pears and sweet potatoes in the fall, as we could pick them up from our local farm stand. Each Sunday, we would enjoy my father's cooking and my mother's baking. It was wonderful, but we had one complaint: when my dad found a recipe that he loved, he would make it over and over again, until we all screamed, "Not again." Fortunately, he listened to our pleas and developed quite an extensive repertoire of recipes. This was how our family favorites were born, and this is one of them that we still make with our own families today.

3 pounds beef chuck
3 tablespoons vegetable oil
3 tablespoons butter
2 tablespoons flour
4 medium onions
½ teaspoon thyme
¼ teaspoon cinnamon
1 pound fresh sweet potatoes, diced or 1 large can
1-2 cloves garlic, minced
½ teaspoon cloves, ground

1 bay leaf
¾ teaspoon salt
½ teaspoon pepper
3 tablespoons raisins
1 teaspoon lemon peel
1½ cups white wine
1½ cups fresh Bartlett pears, diced, or 1 (28 ounce) can pear halves in light syrup (drain pear and reserve 1 cup)

Brown beef in the vegetable oil.

In a separate bowl, mix flour and butter, add it to the beef, and stir.

Add onion, garlic, thyme, cinnamon, and cloves. Stir in salt and pepper, lemon peel, and wine.

Add beef and cook for 1 hour.

Add sweet potatoes, raisins, pears, and pear juice.

Brisket

Chef Kenneth Kohn *(Katz's Deli, New York, NY)*

(Pairs well with Potato Latkes)

5 pound piece first-cut brisket
2 large onions, cut in half, and then sliced into ¼-inch pieces
1½ cups plum tomatoes, diced, or 1 large can crushed tomatoes
1 cup red wine (something rich and deep, such as a nice cabernet)
¼ cup fresh parsley, chopped, or 2 tablespoons dried parsley flakes
2 large garlic cloves, sliced
1 tablespoon Spanish or sweet Hungarian paprika
Salt and pepper to taste

Heat ¼ cup of canola oil in a heavy casserole, and sauté the garlic until brown. While garlic is browning, sprinkle kosher salt, pepper, and paprika to coat the meat on both sides. Remove and discard the garlic. Brown the meat fat-side down. After browning on both sides, add the can of tomatoes and ½ can of water.

Add ½ cup of red wine with the onions and parsley. Cover the casserole and place in a preheated 400°F oven.

After ½ hour, turn the meat and lower the temperature to 325°F.

Cook for an additional 3 hours, turning the meat every ½ hour (if necessary, add water, so, meat is covered three-quarters of the way). During the last half-hour, add the remaining half of wine.

Let the meat stand for 10 minutes before slicing against the grain.

For a complete one-pot dinner, add ¼ pound of potatoes and thinly sliced carrots during the last half-hour. Small, pitted prunes also add a great flavor to the dish.

Planting even one plum tomato plant can sometimes yield as many as fifty tomatoes in September. Not only is this another opportunity to use up all those tomatoes, but this is also a real "grandma" recipe that takes you back in time.

Plum tomatoes, like beefsteak, cherry, and grape tomatoes, are harvested in the late summer. They can remain staked on the vine into the fall, but need to be picked before the first frost. Should an unexpected frost occur, hose down your tomatoes at dawn to remove the ice crystals. Pick them immediately—even if they are green—and after washing, store them in a cool, dry place.

Veggie Tofu Stir-Fry

Monica

Years ago, I unearthed the Macy's *Meals in 30 Minutes* cookbook from the 1940s at a flea market while vacationing in Maine. It was filled with handy recipes for the working woman. It is obvious that many others discovered this book around the time that I did, because there are so many more like it out there today.

I can make meals that are tasty, healthy, and kid-friendly in just twenty minutes. One of our favorites is this veggie and tofu stir-fry. As the days shorten, prep-time needs to fit into our busy fall schedules. I prepare pre-cut broccoli, carrots, and celery on the weekends to use throughout the week.

Extra virgin olive oil to stir-fry
5 cloves garlic, grated
1-inch piece of ginger, grated
1 small bunch scallions, sliced in rounds
and using half of green leaves
1 head broccoli florets, trimmed
1 cup carrots, sliced thin
1 cup snow peas
1 cup celery, sliced thin
Teriyaki sauce
2 packages soft white tofu, cubed
Brown rice

Sauté garlic and ginger briefly.

Add in vegetables in the order written, and stir for 2 minutes.

Add in ⅛ to ¼ cup of teriyaki sauce.

Cook until the vegetables are your desired tenderness.

Fold in cubed tofu, stirring gently so not to break the cubes.

Add a splash or more of teriyaki to suit your taste.

Serve with brown rice.

Eggplant and Ginger over Basmati Rice

Chef John Bochanowicz *(Central Islip, NY)*

3 medium eggplants
4 tablespoons olive oil
2 medium onions
3 cloves garlic, finely chopped
1 ½-inches fresh ginger, peeled and chopped
1 teaspoon cumin seeds
1 medium tomato, diced
1½ tablespoons curry powder
4 chili peppers, finely chopped
1½ cups plain yogurt
1 teaspoon salt
¼ cup fresh cilantro, chopped
3 cups cooked basmati rice

Pierce whole eggplants several times with a fork, and bake at 450°F for about 45 minutes or until tender.

Cool, peel, chop, and then set aside.

Sauté onion, garlic, cumin seeds, and ginger in oil until the onion is soft.

Add curry powder, tomato, and chili peppers, and continue cooking over medium-high heat.

Stir in yogurt, and then add eggplant.

Cover and cook on high for 10 minutes. Add salt.

Reduce the heat to low and cook uncovered for about 5 minutes. Pour over basmati rice, and garnish with cilantro.

Storage Tip

Hot chili peppers are easiest to store once they are dried. You can either hang the whole plant upside down to dry (as you would for herbs) or pick each pepper individually to dry and store, remembering not to rub your eyes. Both ways are effective.

Eggplant Parmigiana Siciliana

Monica

<u>Serves 4-6</u>

With my son off at college, I am now living alone for the first time in thirty-three years, and cooking for one is proving to be a challenge, especially coming from my large Italian family. My freezer is filling up fast with meals that I enjoy once, and then become leftovers with two to four servings packed separately to freeze for future dinners without all the prep-work.

Fresh is always best, but if you are rushing home after a long day at work, you can take several shortcuts to lessen the time that it takes to prepare dinner. Dried herbs and spices, canned tomato products, jarred peppers, artichokes, and olives, pre-grated cheeses, and pre-cut vegetables allow you to enjoy a healthy, home-cooked meal, instead of falling into a take-out routine, which does not allow you to control the ingredients, often resulting in a diet higher in fat, salt, and sugar.

1 large eggplant, thinly sliced lengthwise
1 egg, mixed with splash 1% milk
Seasoned bread crumbs
Extra virgin olive oil
4 cups homemade sauce, or 1 (20 ounce) can tomato puree
Fresh oregano, parsley (or dried), and garlic
2 whole roasted, jarred red peppers
1 large can black olives
1 cup grape tomatoes, sliced
½ cup romano cheese, grated
1 cup mozzarella cheese, shredded

Preheat oven to 350°F.

Dip eggplant into egg and milk mixture, bread, and sauté in extra virgin oil.

Drain excess oil on paper towels before the next step.

Put sauce in the bottom of a 9-inch round baking dish.

Layer in eggplant, sauce, a sprinkle of oregano, parsley, and garlic powder, sliced black olives, roasted red peppers, and grape tomatoes, and a sprinkling of grated parmesan cheese.

Keep layering until you have finished off the eggplant, finally topping off the last layer with mozzarella cheese.

Bake uncovered for 45 minutes.

If you have not used up all of the eggplant that you have harvested in September, it can be blanched and frozen to use in soups, stews, and ratatouille. Basil and parsley from your garden can also be frozen or dried, and used throughout the entire year.

Vegetarian Chili

Monica

I overheard a woman talking to her daughter on her cell phone about what to have for dinner. She said, "I'll make you soup." My eavesdropping turned into interest, and I asked her what kind of soup she was making, thinking that her recipe might be good for this book. She answered, "I use a prepacked chicken soup."

She complained that her daughter had become a vegetarian in the fifth grade, and she was constantly challenged with what to prepare for her. I suggested infusing the packaged soup with chopped vegetables that had been microwaved for five to ten minutes and a handful of beans to make a healthier dish. Fresh carrots, peas, and corn will add vitamins, and fresh corn on the cob can be found at the grocer until mid-October. Try roasting it first, and then add it to your recipe for a richer flavor.

Extra virgin olive oil
4 teaspoons chili powder
1 large onion, sliced
3 garlic cloves, crushed
1 ½ cups diced plum tomatoes, or 1 large can crushed tomatoes
1 large can black beans, drained
1 cup each corn and carrots
2 cups tempeh, crumbled
1 cup raw nuts (pistachios or cashews)
3 cups water
Cilantro or sour cream to garnish

Sauté the onion and garlic in olive oil.

Add the chopped nuts and chili powder.

Add the tomatoes, water, and beans, and cook for 1 hour.

Add the corn and carrots, and after 10 minutes, add the crumbled tempeh.

Salt and pepper to taste. Add the garnish.

Harvest Chili

Kelly Gambardella *(Madison, NJ)*

<u>Serves 12</u>

2 tablespoons olive oil
1 large onion, peeled and chopped
1½ teaspoons ground cumin
1 teaspoon chipotle chili powder (or more, if desired)
2 cups plum tomatoes, diced,
or 2 large cans whole tomatoes in puree
1 medium cauliflower, cut into florets
1 medium sweet potato, peeled and cut in ½-inch cubes
3-4 large carrots, peeled and cut into ¼-inch rounds
1 large green or yellow bell pepper, cored, seeded, and cut into
½-inch dices
½ teaspoon salt
15 ounces any type of bean (I use pink beans)
Sliced scallions for garnish

Sauté onion in olive oil for 5 minutes over medium heat.

Add the cumin and chili powder, cooking for 1 minute.

Stir in the tomatoes, breaking them up with a spoon as needed.

Stir in cauliflower, sweet potatoes, carrots, green pepper, and salt.

Cover and bring to a boil. Reduce the heat and simmer covered for 25 minutes. Stir occasionally.

Add chili beans and simmer for 5 minutes or until vegetables are fork-tender.

Garnish with scallions.

Roast Leg of Lamb

Monica

> Lamb is an acquired taste—many people dislike the aroma.
> I used to liken the flavor to a lambskin coat that I owned as
> a teenager, and would gag at the thought of eating it. Yet I
> always knew that I would like lamb if it was prepared properly.
> So, on a trip to England, we stayed in a farmhouse in the
> countryside, where there was a quaint old restaurant nearby
> that the locals frequented. I boldly ordered the lamb, saying to
> my husband and friends that if I did not like lamb prepared in
> England (where they were famous for it), I would never like it.
> Just as I thought, it was spectacular. I requested an audience
> with the chef, who was kind enough to give me his secret.

Large leg of lamb
1 large stalk fresh rosemary, or dried (about ½ cup)
1 large garlic bulb
⅛ teaspoon salt
2 tablespoons flour
⅛ cup water
1 drop Gravy Master©

Pierce deeply with a sharp knife the entire surface of the lamb, and
stick in garlic cloves that have been cut in thirds.

Sprinkle cut-up sprigs of rosemary over the lamb. Next, sprinkle
salt.

Roast uncovered at 350°F for about 1½ hours.

Make a dark hunter's sauce with the drippings, using flour, water,
a drop of Gravy Master©, and a bit of red wine.

Serve with mashed potatoes and carrots.

Shepherd's Pie

(using Leg of Lamb leftovers)

Monica

> I began making shepherd's pie the very first time that I made a leg of lamb. It seemed like the most obvious thing to do. Many restaurants today use ground beef and canned gravy to make the sauce, with the result being sadly unsatisfying. A true shepherd's pie needs to be made with all the leftovers from the leg of lamb dinner the night before, along with loads of garlic and rosemary, the leftover gravy, potatoes, and vegetables—a shepherd's feast made in minutes. Each time I make this dish, I have to call my nephew, so, he can come and share with my son and I, because he is the only other person in the family who craves it as much as we do.

Roast Leg of Lamb (see page 118)
1 cup carrots
1 cup peas
2 cups gravy
2 cups mashed potatoes, prepared ahead
Parsley to taste, chopped
Paprika to taste

Cut up the lamb into bite-size pieces.

Mix in your carrots and a cup of peas.

Cover with gravy and some water to thin it.

Spread your mashed potatoes over everything. Sprinkle parsley and paprika on top.

Dot with butter and bake uncovered at 350°F for 45 minutes.

If you do not have enough gravy left over, you can always make a stock the night before with the bone after you have cut off all the meat. I give the bone to my dog, and I believe that she thinks that she has died and gone to heaven.

Part IV

DESSERTS

DESSERTS

Dessert: the perfect ending to a perfect meal. For some, dessert is considered the best part of all. Monica's father-in-law would claim he had a second stomach reserved just for dessert, and at least one child in our family now echoes that sentiment at the end of every dinner together. Her mother-in-law, Mary, would bake his favorite dessert, apple pie, almost every week, even into her seventies—that is true love. Following an apple picking sojourn in September, Monica and her husband, Dennis, would deliver a basket full of apples to them, and Mary would start making something special for Dennis' birthday, September 10.

Each fall when Mary Elizabeth's children returned to school, she would volunteer to bake for class parties. Early on, she began collecting cookie cutters in all shapes and sizes for every season and holiday. The one that became her children's favorite was a leaf-shaped design, mainly because she would bake them while they were outside with her husband, raking leaves (with three-quarters of an acre for them to rake, she had ample time to accomplish the task). Her "cut-out" cookies go perfectly with a cup of hot chocolate and are reminiscent of the autumn leaves, especially when dipped in white chocolate and decorated with orange, yellow, and red sugar crystals.

We pour our love into every dessert we make, and then pass it along to those closest to us. Whether it is oatmeal cookies for a school bake sale, cheese cake for a church social, or a gourmet night with your friends, desserts are sweet expressions of love. Of course, dessert is not nutritionally necessary; its value is more emotional than physical. Our bodies do not need delectable treats such as deep, dark chocolate cake dripping with caramel and whipped cream, but part of us is nourished and rejuvenated by the delicious ending to a lovely meal.

It seems to us that dessert has been getting an unfair reputation these days. Watching your sugar intake is one of many popular health trends today. Yet even if you are watching your weight, as long as you keep it in moderation, dessert servings can be just as healthy as the main meal. Incorporating whole wheat flour into your recipes and using fresh fruits and juices are healthy ways of having your cake and eating it, too.

Apple Pie

Mary Carlin *(East Meadow, NY)*

6-7 baking apples (Granny Smith, Cortland, or Rome)
¾ cups sugar
1½-2 teaspoons cinnamon
1 tablespoon flour
Pastry for 9-inch pie (if using Pastry Crust on page 125, omit the nuts)

Preheat oven to 425°F.

Peel and slice apples. Put into a double-dish pie plate evenly.

Mix sugar, cinnamon, and flour together. Sprinkle over apples. Put dots of butter all over the top of the apples.

Add pastry top. Prick open in the center to allow steam to escape.

With a pastry brush, dip into milk or an egg-white wash, and coat surface.

Bake for the first 15 minutes at 425°F, and then reduce the heat to 350 or 375°F for another 30 to 40 minutes or until brown.

Pastry Crust

Lena T. Raiser *(Lynbrook, NY)*

¼ teaspoon salt
2 cups flour
1½ sticks butter
5 tablespoons ice water
2 teaspoons sugar
¼ teaspoon fresh orange or lemon zest
⅓ cup walnuts, finely chopped

Mix flour, salt, sugar, and zest in a bowl or a Cuisinart.

Cut in butter by pulsing, using the blade until crumbs have formed.

While the Cuisinart is running, add ice water, 1 tablespoon at a time, through the chute.

Once the dough has formed into a ball, remove and place in wax paper.

Refrigerate for 1 hour before rolling out.

Fill and bake as directed (you do not have to grease the pie plate).

Fall Apple Crepes with Cinnamon Whipped Cream

Chef Nicole Roarke *(Blue Point, NY)*

Serves 4

> Making crepes is actually easier than people think. It just takes practice. Every good chef throws out their first crepe. Making crepes takes practice, and it is a technique that improves over time.

Crepes

1 cup flour

2 eggs

1 cup milk

¼ teaspoon salt

2 tablespoons melted butter

2 tablespoons sugar

⅛ teaspoon vanilla extract

Dash of cinnamon

2 tablespoons blended oil (see Chef's Tips)

Filling

3 medium fall apples (e.g., Granny Smith or Gala), peeled, cored, and thinly sliced (¼ to ½-inch thick)

¼ cup sugar

Pinch of salt

¼ cup apple brandy

2 tablespoons butter

Zest from 1 medium orange

⅛ teaspoon fresh nutmeg, grated

3 whole cloves

¼ cup mascarpone cheese

1 tablespoon marzipan (almond paste)

½ cup toasted slivered almonds

Crepes

In a large mixing bowl, whisk together flour and eggs. Gradually add in milk, stirring until a smooth batter is formed. Add salt, sugar, vanilla, cinnamon, and melted butter. Allow batter to rest in the refrigerator for at least 2 hours (overnight is best).

Remove from the refrigerator, and whisk until the desired smooth consistency returns. Heat a small non-stick skillet over medium heat. Pour in oil, allow oil to evenly coat the bottom of the pan, pour off the excess oil, and reserve. Pour batter into a skillet, hold handle, remove from the heat, and gently swirl the skillet in circular motions, so, the batter coats the bottom evenly.

Once a thin layer of batter has formed, return to the heat.

When the crepe is ready to flip, small bubbles will appear in the center of the crepe, and the edges will begin to lightly brown (approximately 2 minutes).

Using a heat-resistant rubber spatula, loose crepe, flip over, and cook for approximately one more minute.

Slide crepe out of the skillet onto a holding plate until assembly.

Filling

Heat a large sauté pan on medium-high, and add butter.

Add apples and a pinch of salt, and sauté until apples are tender when pierced with a fork (approximately 4 to 5 minutes).

Sprinkle cinnamon, sugar, nutmeg, and cloves over the apples, and sauté until the sugar begins to dissolve and caramelizes.

Hold pan away from the heat and add apple brandy. Return to the heat. Tilt the edge of the pan toward the flame. Allow liquor to catch fire (flambé).

When flame extinguishes, add almond paste and sauté the apple mixture for an additional 3 minutes.

Remove from the heat, fold in mascarpone and orange zest, and set aside.

Cinnamon Whipped Cream

(See Whipped Cream recipe on page 141)

Add ⅛ teaspoon cinnamon.

Assembly

Lie room-temperature crepes flat.

Place ¼ cup of warm apple filling in the bottom half of the crepe.

Spread evenly with a rubber spatula.

Roll crepe from bottom upward.

Plate crepe seam-side down.

Serve warm with cinnamon whipped cream, sprinkled with toasted, slivered almonds.

Pumpkin Cheesecake with Gingersnap Crust

Chef Maureen Denning *(Snapper Inn, Oakdale, NY)*

Serves 12

Crust

1½ cups ginger snap cookies, crushed

¼ cup finely chopped pecans

¼ cup butter, melted

Filling

4 (8 ounce) packages cream cheese, softened

1 cup sugar

1 teaspoon vanilla

4 eggs

1½ cups canned pumpkin (or equivalent freshly cooked)

1 teaspoon cinnamon

¼ teaspoon nutmeg

Dash of ground cloves

Crust

Combine cookie crumbs, pecans, and butter, and press onto the bottom of a 9-inch spring-form pan. Heat oven to 350°F.

Filling

Beat cream cheese, sugar, and vanilla until smooth and well-blended.

Add eggs one at a time, and beat well after each addition.

Blend in pumpkin and spices, and then mix well. Pour batter into prepared pan and bake for 45 minutes or until the center is almost set. Cool completely and refrigerate for at least 4 hours before serving.

Apple Crisp

Mary Elizabeth

This is a recipe from my mom. She made it often, and we always looked forward to it, especially when served warm with vanilla ice cream or fresh whipped cream on top.

6-7 firm Granny Smith apples, thinly sliced
1 cup flour
1 teaspoon baking powder
1 cup sugar
¾ teaspoon salt
1 unbeaten egg
½ teaspoon vanilla
1 stick sweet butter, melted
¼ teaspoon cinnamon

Place apples in a greased, oblong 6 x 10-inch baking pan, and toss applies with 1 teaspoon of fresh lemon juice.

In a bowl, mix together the flour, baking powder, sugar, salt, vanilla, and egg with a fork until crumbly.

Sprinkle this mixture over the apples.

Top with butter and cinnamon.

Bake for 30-40 minutes at 350°F.

Caramel Sauce

Mary Elizabeth

> This is a great complement to apple crisp, and can also be used for dipping fresh picked apples.

⅓ cup sugar
1 cup light brown sugar
¼ cup each maple syrup and dark corn syrup

In a heavy saucepan, combine all the ingredients. Stir often while you bring it to a boil (approximately 10 to 12 minutes). Cool and drizzle, or dip.

Chevre-Stuffed Baked Apples

Erin Nicosia *(Sayville, NY)*

2 McIntosh apples
1 (4.5 ounce) package chevre
Fresh lemon juice
1½ tablespoons brown sugar
½ teaspoon cinnamon
¼ teaspoon freshly grated nutmeg
¼ cup golden raisins, chopped
¼ cup walnut, chopped

Heat oven to 425°F.

Cut the top off the apples, core, and hollow out the centers. Brush with lemon juice, so, they do not turn brown. In a bowl, combine chevre, brown sugar, cinnamon, nutmeg, golden raisins, and walnuts. Over-stuff the apples, and place in a muffin tin to keep them steady. Bake for about 20 minutes.

Oatmeal Cookies

Mary Elizabeth

1½ sticks sweet butter, softened

1 cup sugar

2 eggs, beaten with a fork

1 cup dried cranberries (or raisins)

5 tablespoons warm water

1 teaspoon each salt, baking soda, and cinnamon

2 cups flour

2 cups instant oatmeal

½ cup chopped walnuts or white chocolate pieces

Place cranberries in warm water and set aside.

Cream butter and sugar until light and fluffy. Add eggs.

Sift together salt, baking soda, cinnamon, and flour.

Add the oatmeal, cranberry and water mixture, and nuts or white chocolate.

Scoop (using a large cookie scoop) onto a greased cookie sheet.

Bake at 400°F for 8 to 10 minutes.

Lunch Box Chronicles

Kathy Acierno *(Sayville, NY)*

My husband Jack was on jury duty for a month, so he was home every morning to help get the kids to school. The girls would bring a snack in a paper lunch-bag, so Jack started writing their names on the bag, and included little pictures on it. This eventually grew into what we called the "Lunch Bag Chronicles." Jack would write elaborate story lines for the girls so they would always have some sort of adventure to look forward to, whether it was driving a herd of hamsters out west or meeting the Great Pumpkin in our local pumpkin patch. Jack has been doing this for several years now, even though my older daughter has graduated to middle school. We have saved all the bags, and hope to make a book out of them some day so the girls can remember the stories when they get older.

Homemade oatmeal cookies were often tucked into their lunch bags. Little did they know just how healthy the oatmeal was! Adding in-season dried cranberries along with the traditional raisins makes for a more colorful cookie.

Peanut Butter Cookies

Mary Elizabeth

½ cup unsalted sweet butter, room temperature
½ cup peanut butter
½ cup granulated sugar
½ cup dark brown sugar
1 egg
½ teaspoon vanilla
1¼ cups flour
¾ teaspoon baking soda
¼ teaspoon salt
12 ounces large milk chocolate discs or chips

Preheat oven to 375°F.

Cream butter, peanut butter, sugars, egg, and vanilla. Sift dry ingredients, and blend into butter mixture. Roll into 2-inch balls, and then roll in granulated sugar.

Place on an ungreased cookie sheet, and bake for 15 minutes. As soon as you remove them, for an extra treat, you can push large milk chocolate chips into the middle.

Cool on racks.

Jam Bars

Lorraine Ott *(Boxford, MA)*

I make this recipe with apple butter. You can also freeze extra berries from your garden and, after the weather has cooled down, start making jams. Any variety of jam complements this cookie bar.

2 sticks unsalted butter, softened
1 cup sugar
1 egg yolk
2 cups flour
¾ cup pecans, finely chopped
12 ounces apple butter or jam
Cinnamon and sugar, optional

Preheat oven to 350°F.

Prepare an 8 x 13-inch baking dish by spraying generously with baking spray. Then place a piece of 8 x 13-inch parchment paper on the bottom of the pan. Spray again.

Cream butter and sugar until light and fluffy, and the color has changed to a pale yellow.

Add yolk, flour, and pecans, and blend well (dough will be soft).

Divide the dough into half, and evenly spread half in the bottom of an 8 x 13-inch baking dish.

Cover with your choice of either apple butter or jam, and then drop the remaining dough by teaspoon-fuls over the jam, spreading carefully with a knife.

If using apple butter, sprinkle with cinnamon sugar.

Bake at 350°F until the tip is golden (about 40 to 45 minutes).

Let it cool thoroughly before cutting into bars.

Apple Fritters

Carol Moore *(Bayport, NY)*

These fritters are a family favorite that remind us of years ago, when we would pick apples at local orchards, using long-handled scoops to pry the fruit off their branches.

1 cup flour
1 teaspoon baking powder
⅛ teaspoon salt
2 eggs
1 teaspoon sugar
⅔ cup milk
1 teaspoon vegetable oil
1 teaspoon brandy
Dash of cinnamon
4 Granny Smith Apples, ½-inch thick slices

Sift dry ingredients. Beat eggs until fluffy. Add milk, oil, brandy, and cinnamon to the eggs. Add flour, and stir only enough to dampen it. Heat oil in a deep skillet to 370°F. Peel and core the apples using an apple corer. Slice ¼ to ½-inch thick. Dip pieces of the apples in batter. Lift out with a fork. Lower carefully into the oil, and fry until delicately brown (about 3 to 5 minutes).

Drain on paper towels. Sprinkle with confectioner's sugar.

Fra Angelica Pie

Monica

> Bowls of fresh mixed nuts still in their shells appear at our grocer's as the weather begins to get cooler. Growing up, it was a challenge to break open the nuts with a nut-cracker. The walnuts would disappear first (also being used for baking), then the pecans and almonds, and followed by the lesser known little, round hazelnuts. Hazelnuts have since moved to the forefront, being used to flavor coffee and liqueurs.

1½ cups vanilla wafers, crumbled
¼ cup shelled, skinned, and chopped hazelnuts
2 tablespoons sugar
6 tablespoons salted butter
1 small packet unflavored gelatin
¼ cup water
1 (8 ounce) package cream cheese
1½ cups confectioner's sugar
¼ cup hazelnut liqueur
2 cups heavy cream, for whipping

Press into a 9-inch pie plate cookie crumbs, three-quarters of the hazelnuts, and then sugar and butter. Bake at 350°F for 8 to 10 minutes. Cool on a wire rack.

Prepare gelatin per package directions, using water, until fully dissolved and cooled. Combine and beat softened cream cheese, confectioner's sugar, and liqueur (in that order) to a smooth consistency.

Beat heavy cream until thick. Add in gelatin and then the cream cheese mixture. Fill the cooled crust and chill well. Toast the remaining chopped hazelnuts, and use to garnish the top just before serving.

> You can use just about any crumbled cookie and nut combination as a pie shell by mixing the crumbs with butter and sugar. Experiment with Oreos, ginger snaps, or graham crackers. Follow the baking directions above.

Pumpkin Nog Pie

Lena T. Raiser *(Lynbrook, NY)*

½ teaspoon salt
¼ cup sugar
1 cup egg nog
½ cup brown sugar
3 egg whites
3 egg yolks, slightly beaten
1 small package unflavored gelatin
½ teaspoon each ground cinnamon and nutmeg
¼ teaspoon ground ginger
1 cup canned pumpkin
9-inch graham cracker crust

In a saucepan over medium heat, combine the gelatin, brown sugar, and spices.

Stir in egg nog, egg yolks, and pumpkin.

Continue to cook and stir over medium heat until the gelatin has dissolved and the mixture comes to a boil.

Remove from the heat and chill until partially set (about 30 minutes).

Beat egg whites until soft peaks form, while gradually adding sugar. Continue to beat until stiff peaks form.

Pour mixture into a prepared crust.

Chill until firm (at least 4 hours).

Graham Cracker Crust

1 cup graham cracker crumbs
½ cup filberts (optional)
3 tablespoons sugar
6 tablepoons melted butter

In a mixing bowl, combine all the ingredients.

Firmly press into a 9-inch pie plate.

Bake at 375°F for 6 to 8 minutes or until the edges are golden brown.

Let it cool on a wire rack while you are preparing the filling.

Apple Spice Cake with Caramel Sauce

Mary Elizabeth

See page 130 for Caramel Sauce recipe.

> Although my dad was affectionately known as a weekend cook in my house (since my mom traditionally did all the baking from scratch), this recipe was the one time my dad deviated from his role. It was he who perfected this recipe that became a favorite of mine in the fall with a cup of chai tea latte.

⅔ cup raisins
2 ounces bourbon
¼ cup applesauce
2 ounces orange juice
1⅓ cups all-purpose flour
⅔ cup cake flour
1 teaspoon baking soda
½ teaspoon each of freshly ground nutmeg and ground cinnamon
¼ teaspoon each ground mace, ginger, and salt
2 sticks unsalted sweet butter
1⅓ cup granulated sugar
2 eggs
2 large Granny Smith apples, cored, peeled, and chopped
½ cup toasted pecans, chopped

Preheat oven to 325°F.

Combine the raisins, bourbon, and orange juice in a small bowl, and let it stand. In a separate bowl, sift the dry ingredients and set aside. Beat butter while slowly adding the sugar until light and fluffy and it becomes pale yellow. Beat in eggs one at a time. Stir in raisin mixture and applesauce. Fold in dry ingredients into the butter mixture until well-incorporated. Stir in apples and pecans. Spoon batter into a 9-inch prepared spring-form pan.

Bake about 1 hour and 15 minutes. Cool on the rack. After you take it out of the spring-form pan, place on a decorative cake dish and drizzle with caramel sauce (see page 130).

Banana Pecan Bread Pudding with Berry Coulis

Chef Roland A. Iadanza *(West Babylon, NY)*

This is a perfect way to use of all of those fresh raspberries you froze in July to use up throughout the year. Dig into your nut dish that often decorates homes throughout the fall. Chefs and kids alike enjoy eating them.

Pudding

2½ cups milk
2½ cups heavy cream
1 cup sugar
4 eggs, beaten
2 teaspoons orange zest
1 teaspoon vanilla extract
24 slices day-old French bread, ½-inch thick
½ cup toasted pecans, shelled

2 bananas, sliced lengthwise
9-inch square cake pan
Confectioner's sugar as needed

Berry Coulis

1 pint raspberries, reserve some for garnish
½ cup sugar
2 tablespoons water

Pudding

Place milk, heavy cream, and sugar on medium heat until sugar has dissolved (about 5 minutes). Place 12 slices of bread in a pan, and put bananas on top. Sprinkle with half of the pecans. Place the 12 remaining bread slices and pecans on top. Add orange zest to the eggs, and then add to the milk mixture, pouring over the bread. Let it sit for 20 minutes. Push bread down with a spatula, and make certain it is well soaked. Place in a water bath at 350°F for 1 hour until set and golden brown. Sprinkle with cinnamon and let it cool; serve with coulis.

Berry Coulis

Warm sugar and water until just before caramelized and has jelly-like consistency. Add berries and combine using a blender. Place coulis on a plate in a pool. Cut bread pudding into squares and place on the sauce. Sprinkle the rim of the plate with cinnamon and confectioner's sugar, placing berries around the plate to garnish. Serve with fresh whipped cream.

Homemade Whipped Cream

> Nothing compares to it. Start with cold beaters and a bowl. You can do this by putting them in the refrigerator while you are assembling your ingredients.

1 pint heavy cream
1 teaspoon vanilla extract
¼ cup confectioner's sugar

Beat all the ingredients until you have achieved the desired consistency.

If you are icing a cake with whipped cream, in order to maintain the stiff peaks, add the following:
1 teaspoon unflavored gelatin
4 teaspoons cold water

Combine unflavored gelatin and water. Let them stand until thick. Then place over low heat, stirring constantly until gelatin dissolves (about 3 minutes).

Bring to room temperature, and slowly add the gelatin mixture when you are starting to beat the cream.

A basic whipped cream is a great foundation. Add ⅛ teaspoon of cinnamon, cocoa powder, or extracts to alter the flavor. You also can be creative and make a savory whipped cream to garnish a soup dish by replacing the sugar with ½ cup of minced fresh dill, for example. Then dollop on your soup before serving.

Plum Torte

Mary Elizabeth

If you are looking for a recipe that comes out perfect every time, look no further. I always have the ingredients at home so I can make it on short notice.

In September, when the plums are in season, wash and dry them thoroughly, and then place them in the freezer. This way, you can make this torte throughout the year. As an alternative to plums, I often substitute a green apple.

1 Italian plum, halved, pitted, and thinly sliced
1 teaspoon each fresh lemon juice, cinnamon, and sugar
2 eggs
1 pinch salt
1 cup sugar
½ cup sweet butter, softened
1 cup flour
1 teaspoon baking powder

Preheat oven to 350°F.

Place fruit in a bowl, and coat with lemon juice and 1 teaspoon of sugar and cinnamon. Set aside.

Cream butter and sugar.

Add the rest of the ingredients and beat well.

Spoon into a greased 9-inch, spring-form pan. Place fruit on top in a circle design.

Bake at 350°F for 1 hour.

Toasted Butter Pecan Cake

Pastry Chef Tuesday Jordan *(Hempstead, NY)*

> Here is a recipe that was passed down to me by my grandmother.
> It was reserved for the fall. To make it more festive, she would
> adorn it by placing leaf-shaped cookie cutters on top after it was
> iced, and generously sprinkled sugar crystals in each one with
> a different fall hue: yellow, red, and orange.

2 cups pecans, finely chopped
1 cup butter
¼ cup butter, melted
2 cups sugar
4 eggs
3 cups flour
2 teaspoons baking powder
½ teaspoon salt
1 cup milk
1 teaspoon vanilla

Frosting
8 ounces butter
16 ounces shortening
2 pounds confectioner's sugar
2 teaspoons vanilla extract
⅔ cup pecans
¼ cup plus 1 tablespoon heavy cream

Combine pecans and ¼ cup of butter, and spread on a shallow baking sheet.

Toast in oven at 350°F for 20 minutes.

Set aside ⅔ cup of toasted pecans.

In a large mixing bowl, cream sugar and butter until fluffy and light in color.

Add eggs one at a time, beating well after each addition.

Sift the dry ingredients together, and add to sugar mixture.

Alternating with the milk, add vanilla and stir in 1⅓ cups of toasted pecans. Pour batter into 3 greased and floured 9-inch round cake pans, and bake at 350°F for 20 to 25 minutes. Remove from pans, and cool on a rack.

Frosting

Cream shortening and butter by beating for 2 minutes. If available, use a paddle attachment.

Add sugar. Mix for 6 minutes until the lumps disappear. Scrape down the sides and bottom of the bowl.

Add cream and vanilla. Mix for 2 minutes.

Add in pecans, and frost the cake.

Chocolate Chip Cake

Lorraine Ott *(Boxford, MA)*

I could never forget going to the house of my husband's friend for Halloween parties. She only hosted it every other year because she had to start decorating for it a full month in advance. Needless to say, as the years went by, she added to her collection of Halloween props, complete with a coffin and a table on which you were invited to feel various fake organs. I would always make what became known as the "Spider Cake." It was actually my friend Lorraine's chocolate chip cake recipe, but I topped it with ganache (see page 146). The beauty of the shiny, smooth icing was that it made a perfect surface to decorate. I would take white gel and pipe it out in the shape of a spider web. To get the full effect, I also placed a plastic spider in the web, and when I would cut into the cake, I would tell the kids that the chips were spider eggs.

(Story by Mary Elizabeth)

1 stick butter, softened
1 (8 ounce) package cream cheese, softened
1¼ cups sugar
2 eggs
¼ cup milk
1 teaspoon vanilla
2 cups flour
1 teaspoon baking powder
½ teaspoon baking soda
6 ounces semisweet chocolate chips

Cream together butter, cream cheese, and sugar.

Add eggs, alternating milk with vanilla and sugar.

Add dry ingredients, and beat until blended.

Stir in chocolate chips (batter will be thick). Pour into 2 (8-inch) round pans.

Bake for 40 minutes at 350°F.

Ganache

16 ounces good-quality semisweet or milk chocolate bar, chopped

1⅓ cups heavy cream

4 tablespoons sweet butter, cut into tablespoons

Place the chocolate in a large bowl.

In a saucepan over medium heat, heat the cream and butter until the mixture just comes to a boil.

Pour the hot cream mixture over the chocolate pieces. Let it stand for 1½ minutes.

With a hand-held whisk, mix until smooth. Note: start in the middle of the bowl and work your way out, pulling in more of the chocolate mixture as you widen the circle. It will take several minutes to get to the right consistency.

Let the ganache cool for 15 to 20 minutes before icing.

Makes enough to ice 1 cake or 24 cupcakes.

Zachary's Favorite Cupcakes

Lili Papadakis *(Plainview, NY)*

A healthy alternative to Chocolate Chip Cake (see page 145)

4 tablespoons soy margarine
½ cup sugar
1 cup soy milk
1 teaspoon vanilla
1½ cups flour
½ teaspoon salt
1 teaspoon baking soda
1 teaspoon baking powder

Frosting
1 pound confectioner's sugar
½ stick soy margarine
1 teaspoon vanilla
2 tablespoons soy milk

Preheat oven to 400°F.

Using an electric mixer, blend margarine and sugar until creamy.

Slowly mix in soy milk (it will not blend in, this is normal).

Stir in vanilla.

Add dry ingredients, and mix into a dough consistency.

Spoon into cupcake holders, and bake for 18 to 20 minutes.

Cool cupcakes and frost and decorate, or pour into 2 greased and floured cake pans.

Frosting

Blend until creamy. To make chocolate frosting, sprinkle plain cocoa into the frosting once it is blended.

"Cut-Out" Cookies

2 sticks salted butter, room temperature
¾ cup sugar
½ teaspoon salt
1½ teaspoons vanilla
1 large egg, room temperature
2 teaspoons heavy cream
2¼ cups flour

Preheat oven to 350°F.

Cream butter and sugar by beating them together for 3 minutes until you see a change in the color and consistency (it should be light yellow and fluffy).

Beat in vanilla, egg, and milk.

Add flour and salt until it is blended.

Refrigerate for 1 to 2 hours before rolling out.

Bake for 10 minutes.

Variation

For a spiced cookie version, sift the following spices with the flour: ½ teaspoon each of ground cardamom, ginger, allspice, and cinnamon.

Tips for a Well-Stocked Pantry

It is always best to use fresh vegetables, meats, and fish, but sometimes you may have to rely on your stored ingredients when pressed for time. Try to keep the following items stocked in your pantry and freezer, so you can cook up a tasty and healthy meal any time. It is also a good idea to stock up when these items are on sale at your supermarket. Always remember to check the expiration date on sale items.

Basics for a Quick Meal

In the Pantry: whole wheat pasta (different shapes and sizes), brown rice, oatmeal, and other cereals, seasoned bread crumbs, stuffing mix, several varieties of beans (dried and canned), canned tomatoes (whole, crushed, pureed, and paste), Gravy Master©, chicken and beef stocks, canned milk, dried mushrooms, and various nuts

Dried spices: garlic and onion powders and pieces, crystallized and ground ginger, chili powder, paprika, cumin, whole and ground cloves, cinnamon, nutmeg, curry powder, garam masala, coriander, and different kinds of salt and pepper

Dried herbs: oregano, parsley, dill, ground and whole rosemary, basil, cilantro, mint, sage, bay leaves, and thyme

In the Freezer: several kinds of vegetables and fruits including peppers, onions, celery, cherries, berries, bananas, and peaches, frozen juices from citrus fruits kept in ice trays, pizza dough, cheese, butter, cookie dough, leftover stock (vegetable, fish, and chicken), sauces, and bits of meats, peeled shrimp, and fish fillets

In the Refrigerator: lemon, lime, and orange juice, any leftovers from open bottles of wine, beer, and champagne to use in a recipe, capers, relish, sun-dried tomatoes, olives, relish, horseradish, marmalade and·jams, variety of bottled sauces for flavoring including chili sauce, hoisin, teriyaki, soy and barbeque

Fall is for Herbs

Here is a sampling of basics for every herb garden:

- Basil
- Chives
- Coriander (also known as cilantro)
- Dill
- Mint
- Oregano
- Parsley
- Rosemary
- Thyme

Most of us are ambitious gardeners, and we end up buying and growing more herbs than we can possibly use. So, before you start planting, be sure to carefully plan how much you will need to grow.

Your herbs should be harvested in the fall before the first frost. Once you bring them in, you will need to decide whether you will be using them within the next week or not. If you will not be using them right away, they can be dried for use in the winter months. Place chopped basil or parsley leaves or whole thyme or rosemary on a plate. Set aside in a cool, dry place for several days, and then store them in a plastic container in the refrigerator. For shorter-term storage of basil, parsley, and cilantro, you can trim the ends, place in a glass with an inch of water, and place on the counter at room temperature for up to a week.

For chives, thyme, and rosemary, loosely cover the unrinsed herbs in plastic wrap, and place in the warmest part of the refrigerator or in a large plastic bag with a crumbled paper towel. Rinse them immediately before using.

Growing Your Own Food

Healthy living does not mean giving up good food and great flavor. Simply eating unprocessed food and employing healthy cooking methods will put you on track for better overall health. Serving fresh garlic, green, leafy vegetables like spinach and kale, herbs like basil and parsley, and using extra virgin olive oil for sautéing and salad dressings are all great ways to improve and maintain a healthier lifestyle.

Growing some of your own vegetables and fruits has the added benefits of saving money and increasing quality family time by working together in the garden. Blueberries and raspberries are easy to grow, and can be great options for beginning gardeners. Monica's Italian garden is comprised of herbs such as oregano, basil, and parsley, along with cherry, plum, and beefsteak tomatoes, eggplant, green and red peppers, and zucchini. Harvest the peppers, eggplant, tomatoes, and zucchini through mid-autumn. She also grows broccoli, cucumber, lettuce, and additional herbs, including mint, chives, sage, dill, rosemary, cilantro (which, when it goes to seed, results in coriander), and lavender. We eat what is most plentiful as it is picked, and then prepare and freeze the rest for future use.

It is important to pick at just the right time to elicit the maximum flavor, texture, and nutritional value. You can get the most vitamins and minerals from your produce by using them as soon after harvesting as possible. Essential vitamins and minerals enable our bodies to function properly, which helps us to live longer, more productive lives. It is also important to store your precious fruits and vegetables properly, being careful not to bruise them while picking, because they will spoil more quickly.

Chef's Tips: Kitchen Must-Haves
by Chef Nicole Roarke

When arriving home from the grocery store, spend an additional twenty minutes properly storing your food. Place a colander in the sink and a cutting board on the counter, and then grab your plastic storage containers. Begin washing the vegetables and fruit in the colander, using your discretion on which items can be left whole (such as apples), while others can be "broken down" (heads of broccoli can be cut into florets). Chefs refer to "breaking down" as the trimming and cutting of ends, roots, leaves, skins, outer layers, and stalks. By saving the unusable celery roots, carrot peels, and pepper stems, for instance, you can prepare your own vegetable and chicken stock at a later date.

By purchasing whole vegetables, or buying in bulk and breaking them down yourself, you save money and can control the quality of your homemade stock, rather than using store-bought stock. When you are about to prepare a recipe, the majority of your vegetables are now ready. This initial twenty minutes spent storing your produce will help you save time the day before preparing for dinner, parties, or events.

For example, after washing the head of broccoli, cut the florets and store them in the refrigerator in a plastic container or a large plastic bag so it is ready to eat. Keep the stems and stalks in a large bowl designated as your "stock bin." Continue breaking down the rest of your vegetables so your refrigerator is filled with cleaned, cut, and easily accessible vegetables, as well as a full "stock bin" for making homemade stock.

It is also helpful to use this method when purchasing and storing your proteins. Rather than putting ten pounds of chicken in your refrigerator (which may spoil before you can use it), open the package and individually wrap each piece and place them in large freezer bags. Determine how much to store in your refrigerator for immediate use, and place the remaining individual bags in the freezer to be taken out for a later date.

Basic Recipe for Vegetable Stock

Makes 2 quarts

1. Fill a stock pot or large sauce pot with vegetable trimmings from your stock bin.
2. Be sure to include 1 yellow onion, 2 carrots, and 1 bunch of celery, fresh herbs, including, but not limited to, bay leaf, thyme, parsley stems, rosemary, and peppercorns.
3. Add cold water, just covering the vegetables, bring to a boil, and immediately reduce to a simmer. Simmer for 1 hour.
4. Remove from heat and let cool for 30 minutes.
5. Strain contents through a colander, and then a second time through a fine mesh strainer called a chinois.
6. If you prefer a darker stock, add 2 tablespoons of tomato paste and any tomato trimmings you have.

Note: Most chefs agree not to salt the stock. Use the stock as a basic foundation for a soup or sauce that can be further flavored or salted later on. This way, you can control the amount of salt that goes into the finished product.

Basic Recipe for Chicken Stock

Makes 2 quarts

1. In a large stock pot, fill with raw or cooked chicken, gizzards, bones, trimmings, and neck—do not use internal organs (e.g., liver or kidneys).
2. Add cold water to just cover the chicken parts and vegetable trimmings from your stock bin. Be sure to include 1 yellow onion, 2 carrots, and 1 bunch of celery, and fresh herbs, including but not limited to, bay leaf, thyme, parsley stems, rosemary, and peppercorns.
3. Bring to a boil and allow to simmer for at least 1 hour, but no more than 2 hours.
4. Remove from heat. Allow it to cool for 30 minutes.
5. Strain contents through a colander, and then a second time through a fine mesh strainer called a chinois. If the stock is for immediate use, skim off any excess fat from the top of the stock with a large spoon or ladle, and discard. If the stock is to be used at a later

date, once cooled in the refrigerator, the fat will rise to the top and solidify, which can easily be removed with a large spoon before use.

6. If you prefer a dark stock, coat the chicken bone with vegetable oil and roast in an oven for approximately 20 to 30 minutes at 350 °F until a brown color is achieved. Then proceed as above, but you should include an 8-ounce can of tomato paste and any tomato trimmings that you have.

Now, it is up to you to season with salt to taste. Otherwise, use as a flavor foundation.

Mise en place

Mise en place [MEEZ-ahn-plahs] is a French term that literally means "setting in place." *Mise en place* refers to a chef's set-up of essential ingredients and tools that are necessary to begin the actual cooking process. Before beginning any recipe, it is important to:

1. Have all the ingredients and equipment readily accessible.
2. Read the entire recipe and make sure that you understand all of the instructions and steps you need to follow.

If your *mise en place* is set out and organized right in front of you, it allows for a steady flow of production. Essentially, organization leads to less error. For most professional and at-home chefs, our *mise en place* consists of:

- Kosher salt: Keep readily accessible in a small finger pot.
- Freshly cracked black pepper: Keep in a refillable pepper mill with whole black peppercorns.
- Blended oil: Olive oil alone tends to be strong in flavor, expensive, and cannot withstand high cooking heat. By adding oil such as vegetable, canola, or soybean, you can create your own blended oil. I follow a three to one ratio: three parts light or neutral oil such as canola or vegetable (corn or soybean work just as well) to one part extra virgin olive oil.

3. Flour/corn starch: Not only are flour or corn starch essential for baking, they oftentimes act as a thickening agent, if necessary.

Roux is equal parts flour to fat. For example, 1 cup of all-purpose flour to 1 cup of melted butter. Whisk together over low heat until it is sandy in color and similar to peanut butter in consistency. By this time, all the raw flour taste is cooked out. This takes approximately 5 minutes. By adding a roux to a sauce or soup and bringing it to a boil, you can thicken it instantly.

Slurry is a mix of ½ cup of corn starch with ¼ to ½ cup of cold water until a heavy cream consistency is reached. Bring your recipe (e.g., sauce or soup) to a boil and whisk in the slurry. Return to a simmer (5 to 7 minutes). If you add corn starch directly to your recipe, it will clump and not alter the thickness, which is why it is necessary to mix the corn starch with water or any flavorful liquid (such as wine, stock, or juice) ahead of time before adding it to your recipe.

4. Sugar/honey: Just as a pinch of salt is added to almost all baking recipes to bring out the sweetness and balance the flavor, I add a pinch of sugar or tablespoon of honey to my savory soups and sauces. I believe it creates a well-rounded depth of flavor.

5. Roasted garlic: There are two ways to roast garlic:
   - Cut a quarter off the top of a whole bulb of garlic.
   - Drizzle with oil, salt, and pepper.
   - Place bulb in the center of a large, square piece of aluminum foil. Bring the corners up around the bulb and pinch close at the top.
     Place foil onto a sheet tray.
   - Roast "low and slow" at 300 °F for 45 minutes until fragrant and soft.
   - Remove from the oven, open foil, and allow to cool.
   - For use, squeeze individual cloves out of the bulb.

   OR
   - Place 1 cup of whole, peeled garlic cloves in a medium sauce pot.
   - Pour blended oil over the garlic just until it is covered (approximately 2 cups).
   - Place pot over medium to low heat (the oil should be lower than a simmer).
   - After 20 to 30 minutes, the garlic should be soft, fragrant, and slightly gold in color.

- Allow garlic to cool.

6. Blended herb oil
   - Place 1 cup of tightly packed fresh herbs (such as basil, dill, or a combination such as ½ cup of sage and ½ cup of thyme) in a blender or food processor. Be sure to use only the leaves, and discard all stems.
   - Add 1 teaspoon of kosher salt and $1/8$ teaspoon of freshly cracked black pepper.
   - Pulse herbs, salt, and pepper to rough chop.
   - Add blended oil to cover and puree.

You can either leave the herbs in the oil for a stronger flavor and more rustic appearance, or you can strain the oil with a fine mesh strainer or chinois (cone-shaped strainer). The oil retains a beautiful light-green color, and should be very fragrant and delicious. Use as a dipping oil for fresh bread, as a dressing for a fresh mozzarella and plum tomato salad, as a drizzle on a plate, or on top of a pureed soup. You can also add the herb oil to mayonnaise to create an herb aioli for potato salad. Add to cream and serve over pasta. The possibilities are endless and always delicious.

Baker's Tips

Have you ever tasted something that you absolutely loved, but when you got the recipe and attempted to reproduce it, you could not come up with the same results? Baking is a precise science. You cannot deviate from the directions—when they say "do not over beat," they mean it. If you follow the directions exactly, you will be surprised at the results.

Read your recipe from start to finish. Every baker can tell you a story of leaving out a key ingredient when they were distracted or multitasking, as many of us do. Or, after beginning your recipe, you get to the end and read that it must chill for three hours, and your guests are arriving to eat in one hour.

Preheat the oven. A good rule of thumb to follow is to turn your oven on before you move on to the next step in the recipe so that by the time you are ready to put the pan in the oven, it will be at the correct temperature. It is also a good idea to hang an oven thermometer from the rack, and periodically check that the internal temperature matches the one that you set.

Mise en place **all your ingredients before you begin.** It is important to use your measuring cup for flour, but remember to level it off and use a knife to tap the top of the cup, making sure that it settles.

Use a cooking scale to weigh your ingredients.

Eggs and butter must be brought to room temperature. If you see this in your recipe, you should start with this step first. Take the amount of butter you need, cut it into tablespoons, and put it on your counter. The room air will soften it up, so when it is time to actually start the recipe, it has come to the perfect consistency.

Prepare your baking pan(s). I can still hear my chef instructor saying, "Spray —paper—spray." If only I knew this one little baker's tip, all my baking pans would not be black now. All you need is baking spray (you can find it in the aisle with the baking ingredients) and parchment paper. Cut the paper to the size of your baking pan. Spray the pan generously, put down the paper evenly, being careful not to overlap, and then spray generously again. After you finish baking, you will see how easily your baked goods will come out of the pan. You will find that the paper easily peels off. Consider treating yourself to three good-quality cookie sheets, so while two are baking in the oven, you can be scooping the cookies onto the next one.

Baker's cooling racks. Cool everything on a rack thoroughly before attempting to take it out of the pan (have at least three on hand).

Buy good-quality chocolate, vanilla, and cinnamon. Whenever I shop, I make sure to stop in the baking aisle of the store to buy chocolate when it is on sale to keep my pantry well-stocked.

Use fresh spices and herbs whenever possible. It will make all the difference in the taste.

Beat butter and sugar. When a recipe says to beat butter and sugar, always follow these directions to make sure it comes out perfect each time: first, the butter must be softened or at room temperature, which only takes about fifteen minutes. Then beat it for three minutes with a Kitchen Aid mixer set at number "6" (set the timer when you do this step, and after a minute-and-a-half, stop to scrape the sides of the bowl with a spatula), or until you see a change in the color and consistency (it should be light-yellow and fluffy). After a while, you will just know by looking at it.

Oil cloth. Rolling dough on an oil cloth makes it even easier to peel it off the cloth and slide it onto the pie plate. All you need is a twenty-by-twenty-inch piece of good-quality oil cloth. Draw an eight, nine, and ten-inch circle in the middle using a permanent marker. This way, when you need to roll out dough for a nine-inch pie plate, your template will be handy.

Baking Must-Have Ingredients:

- Salt, baking powder, baking soda, and instant oatmeal
- All-purpose (also known as "AP") flour
- All types of chocolate—white, dark, semisweet, and unsweetened
- Salted, sweet butter
- Eggs

- Whole milk and heavy cream
- Vanilla
- Sugars—confectioner's sugar, white, granulated sugar, and dark brown sugar
- Molasses, dark and light corn syrups

Baking Must-Have Equipment:

- Zester
- Several sets of individual measuring cups and measuring spoons
- Two Pyrex measuring cups
- Small preparation bowls or Pyrex custard cups
- Three each of cutting boards, good-quality cookie sheets, and cooling racks
- One large and one small cookie scoop
- Variety of cookie cutters (seasonal and shapes)
- Four mixing bowls (of various sizes)
- Cuisinart
- Hand-mixer
- Whisk, spatulas (all sizes), wooden spoons, and a ruler
- Good-quality knife (for chopping nuts and chocolate)
- Hand-sifter
- Pastry brush

Menu Planner

by Chef Nicole Roarke and Mary Elizabeth

One of the first things that you should do when starting to plan a menu for a special event or holiday is to get out all of your favorite cookbooks, recipe file boxes, and any other recipe collections that you have created.

Here is the process for recipe collection that Mary Elizabeth developed over the past thirty years: as I go through the culinary magazines that I receive each month, I fold over any pages with recipes that I want to try. After I have thoroughly savored the magazine, I tear out those pages and place them into an accordion folder, which contains tabs for each course (breakfast, lunch, snack, dinner, dessert, etc.).

The first time that I try a new recipe, I typically follow it exactly as written. If I like the recipe and it is well-received by my family or company, it gets pulled out of the accordion folder and is typed up on my computer, where I add any notes that I took along the way (e.g., a different technique that I used, a short-cut, or variations in ingredients). Then I file it on my hard drive in a recipe file with subfolders for each course. I love to share recipes with others, so I can easily send it to them in an e-mail.

Afterwards, I print it out and place it in my "Keeper" binder with tabs for each course. My binder is not fancy, but I made sure to use one that has a clear plastic sleeve on the front. When I start prepping to make a recipe, I pull it out of the binder, place it under the plastic sleeve, and stand it on my counter. Needless to say, the plastic sleeve inevitably gets splattered, but can easily be wiped off with a sponge, keeping the recipe intact so it can be filed away again. This process continues as I often find myself making notes on the recipes (for example, if I find a particular brand that makes a difference in the flavor, or I substitute or add a new ingredient).

When planning a menu, you should keep in mind the following key questions:

How many guests will I be expecting?
Whether it is a party of fifty or a dinner for you and your spouse, the number of guests is important to determine before grocery shopping for your food and fare.

What is my budget?
Certain food items are more expensive than others, so planning meals with lower-cost ingredients will help you stick to your budget without sacrificing quality.

What is my concept or theme?
Like great music, each component of a great dish should be in harmony with one another. The whole meal should make sense. If it is a Mexican fiesta, Italian pasta night, or a New Year's Eve cocktail party, you should keep the menu items synchronized to ensure that the flavors will mesh well together. Creating a concept or theme for your menu and event will keep you (the chef) focused within these guidelines, and prevent you from feeling overwhelmed. Balancing flavors, colors, and textures goes hand-in-hand with deciding which recipes complement each other.

Do my guests have any dietary restrictions or limitations?
For example, one of your guests may be a vegetarian, diabetic, or is allergic to nuts or shellfish. Knowing what your guests can and cannot have will guarantee an enjoyable meal. It may also be helpful to keep notes on an index card in your recipe box where you list guest names and any dietary restrictions, as well as their likes and dislikes.

Finally, do not overwhelm your guests. Keep it simple and offer several choices, especially when planning a buffet. To give yourself more time with your guests, be sure to have everything out before anyone arrives. Attractively display several cold appetizers and dips, decorative Sterno dishes with meat and pasta entrées, and a large salad and basket of bread that complements your theme. You may also want to have the coffee urn ready to plug in, along with a selection of teas. For dessert, offer choices including fruit, chocolate, and something plain such as pound cake or sugar cookies.

Years of hosting many dinner parties and family gatherings have gone into learning what goes well together. Below you will find menus that you can use, which are comprised of recipes from each chapter, to form a complete menu for you and your guests. Enjoy.

Seven Days of Menus

	Breakfast/Brunch	Lunch	Entrées/Sides	Desserts
Sunday	Autumnal Crepes (pg 4) Sausage and Egg Strata (pg 20) Zucchini Bread(pg 9) Fresh Pappardelle with Roasted Eggplant (pg 64)	Tomato Basil Soup (pg 50)	Mom's Sauerbraten (pg 81) Red Cabbage with Apples (pg 83) Dumplings (pg 77) Applesauce (pg 13)	Applesauce Loaves (pg 12)
Monday	Harvest Muffins (pg 22)	Pumpkin Bisque (pg 49) Spinach Salad (pg 47)	Shepherd's Pie (pg 119)	Apple Crisp (pg 129)
Tuesday	Fruit Granola with Yogurt (pg 17)	Roasted Red Pepper Hummus (pg 32) Taboulleh with Veggies (pg 31)	Penne and Roasted Butternut Squash with Sage and Chevre (pg 87)	Banana Pecan Bread Pudding with Berry Coulis (pg 140)
Wednesday	Eggs with Homemade Breakfast Sausage (pg 21)	Homemade Peanut Butter (pg 37) Backyard Grape Jam (pg 36)	Garden Herbed Seared Chicken with Red Pepper Sauce (pg 99)	Plum Torte (pg 142)
Thursday	French Toast (pg 6) Warm Fruit Compote (pg 7)	Curried Chicken Salad on a Bed of Greens (pg 30)	Grandma Reger's Meatloaf (pg 106) Mushroom Gravy (pg 107) German Potato Pancakes (pg 108)	Chevre-Stuffed Baked Apples (pg 131)
Friday	Zucchini Bread with Cream Cheese (pg 9)	Spanakopita or Spinach Pie (pg 38) Greek Salad (pg 40)	Seared Maine Diver Sea Scallops (pg 92) Bibb Salad with Sage Vinaigrette (pg 43)	Pumpkin Cheesecake with Gingersnap Crust (pg 128)
Saturday	Frittata (pg 16) Popovers (pg 8)	Homemade Pizza (pg 65) Caesar Salad (pg 46)	Roast Leg of Lamb (pg 118) Roasted Potatoes (pg 96) Roasted Curried Squash (pg 98)	Toasted Butter Pecan Cake (pg 143)

Request for Future Submissions

We have thoroughly enjoyed collecting these stories. As we received each story and recipe, we would anxiously read through and decide if it could be included in our book. We knew it would be included if it evoked in us the emotions and memories that come to mind when we remembered our own traditions. We have reached out to family, friends, neighbors, and colleagues, and now we are reaching out to you, our readers. We would love to have you share your stories with us.

To do so, please send us the following information and e-mail your story to us at traditionsus@yahoo.com. Please include your name, e-mail address, city, and state.

There is no word count or previous writing experience necessary, and we only require one rule: you write from your heart.

Thank you,

Mary Elizabeth and Monica

Index

Chicken

 Athenian Chicken with Fresh Herbs, 101

 Chicken and Bean Burritos, 34

 Garden Herbed Seared Chicken with Red Pepper Sauce, 99

 Hearty Chicken Pot Pie, 109

Chili

 Harvest Chili, 117

 Vegetarian Chili, 116

Cheesecake; Pumpkin Cheesecake with Gingersnap Crust, 128

Chocolate Chip Cake, 145

Cookies

 Jam Bars, 134

 "Cut-Out" Cookies, 148

 Oatmeal Cookies, 132

 Peanut Butter Cookies, 133

Compote; Warm Fruit, 7

Cream Cheese Icing, 14

Crepes

 Autumnal Crepes, 4

 Fall Apple Crepes with Cinnamon Whipped Cream, 126

Curried Butternut Squash Soup, 53

Curried Chicken Salad, 30

"Cut-Out" Cookies, 148

Dumplings, 77

Eggplant

 Eggplant and Ginger over Basmati Rice, 113

 Eggplant Parmigiana Siciliana, 114

Fall Apple Crepes with Cinnamon Whipped Cream, 126

Fall Stew, 110

Fra Angelica Pie, 136

French Toast, 6

Fresh Pappardelle with Roasted Eggplant, Ricotta Salata & Pine Nuts, 64

Frittata, 16

Fruit Granola, 17

Garden Herbed Seared Chicken with Red Pepper Sauce, 99

Ganache, 146

German Potato Pancakes, 108

Gnocchi with Brown Butter Sauce, 97
Graham Cracker Crust, 138
Grandma Raymond's Spaetzle Soup, 58
Grandma Reger's Meatloaf, 106
Grandpa's Sauerkraut, 80
Granola, Fruit, 17
Gravy; Mushroom, 107
Greek Salad, 40

Harvest Chili, 117
Harvest Muffins, 22
Hash; Roasted Root Vegetable Hash with Crispy Pancetta and Poached Eggs, 10
Herbed Angel Hair with Wilted Radicchio, 84
Hearty Chicken Pot Pie, 109
Homemade Breakfast Sausage, 21
Homemade Peanut Butter, 37
Homemade Pizza, 65
Homemade Whipped Cream, 141
Hummus; Red Pepper, 32

Italian Meatballs, 104

Jam
    Backyard Grape Jam, 36
    Jam Bars, 134

Lettuce Boats Filled with Corn Salsa, 33
Linguini with Little Neck Clams & Vegetables, 91
Lobster Salad on Garlic Crostini with Mango Salsa, 41

Maple Walnut Butter, 15
Mary's Beef "Ghoulash", 75
Meat
    Italian Meatballs, 104
    Meatloaf; Grandma Reger's, 106
    Mom's Sauerbraten, 81
    Pan-Seared Duck Tacos with Habañero Mole and Tomatillo Salsa, 72
    Roast Leg of Lamb, 118
Minestrone Soup, 48
Mom's Old Fashioned Zucchini Bread, 9
Mom's Sauerbraten, 81
Moroccan Spiced Carrot Soup, 62

Quesadillas; Smokey, Cheesy Quesadillas with Sweet Corn Relish, 70
Quiche; Swiss Chard, Leak & Gruyere Quiche, 18

Red Cabbage with Apples, 83
Red Pepper and Goat Cheese Crostini, 28
Red Pepper Hummus, 32
Refrigerator Soup, 60
Roast Leg of Lamb, 118
Roasted Curried Squash, 98
Roasted Potatoes, 96
Roasted Red Pepper Lasagna, 88
Roasted Root Vegetable Hash with Crispy Pancetta and Poached Eggs, 10

Salads
    Autumn Squash Salad, 44
    Bibb Salad with Sage Vinaigrette, 43
    Caesar Salad, 46
    Chai Lentil Salad, 42
    Curried Chicken Salad, 30
    Greek Salad, 40
    Lobster Salad on Garlic Crostini with Mango Salsa, 41
    Spinach Salad, 47
Salmon; Baked and Creamed Spinach Provençal, 94
Salsa; Lettuce Boats Filled with Corn Salsa, 33
Sauerbraten; Mom's, 81
Sauerkraut; Grandpa's, 80
Sausage and Egg Strata, 20
Sausage; Homemade Breakfast, 21
Seafood
    Seafood and Zucchini Medley a la Italy, 95
    Seared Maine Diver Sea Scallops over Butternut Squash Risotto
    with Pancetta & Fresh Sage, 92
Shepherd's Pie, 119
Smokey Cheesy Quesadillas with Sweet Corn Relish, 70
Soup
    Autumn Squash Soup with Gruyere Cheese Gratin, 56
    Curried Butternut Squash Soup, 53
    Grandma Raymond's Spaetzle Soup, 58
    Minestrone Soup, 48
    Moroccan Spiced Carrot Soup, 62
    Onion Soup, 51

Resources

A heartfelt thanks goes out to our contributing chefs for sharing their inspiration and their works of art:

Chef Phil Andriano, www.chefsdiet.com
Paula Gottlieb Herman, www.lilchefs.com
Chef Roland A. Iadanza, www.pastapeopleny.com
Pastry Chef Tuesday Jordan, http://treatsbydesign.com
Chef Ashton Colleen Keefe, www.diaryofasweettooth.com
Carol Moore, www.cookingfreak.com
Nini Ordoubadi, www.taytea.com
Chef Nicole Roarke, www.nrcatering.com
Lee Stevens, http://letleecook.com
Polly Talbott, CCP, www.alacartecs.com
Chef Tricia Wheeler, www.ediblecolumbus.com
Chef Maureen Denning, www.thesnapperinn.com
Chef Joe DiNicola, www.latavolasayville.com
Chef Meredith Machemer, www.greyhorsetavern.com

Our Favorite Culinary Websites

Epicurious: Seasonal Ingredients
www.epicurious.com/articlesguides/seasonalcooking/farmtotable/seasonalingredientmap

USDA Farmers Market Search
apps.ams.usda.gov/FarmersMarkets

Taste of Home
www.tasteofhome.com

Recipes & Local Food Resources

Chicago Green City Market
www.chicagogreencitymarket.org

Epicurious
www.epicurious.com

Healthy Dining
www.healthydining.org

Slow Food USA

www.slowfoodusa.org

Food Network

www.foodnetwork.com

BigOven: Fall Recipes

www.bigoven.com/recipes/tag/Fall

Fruit from Washington: Recipe Quantity Calculator

www.fruitfromwashington.com/Recipes/scale/recipeconversions.php

AllFoodBusiness.com: Cooking Conversion Calculators

www.allfoodbusiness.com/calculators_online.php

My Recipes

My Recipes

My Traditions

My Traditions